THE POWER OF CROSS

Worship Song ... st's Sacrifice

ISBN 978-1-4234-9252-8

HAL•LEONARD®
CORPORATION

7777 W. BLUEMOUND RD. P.O. BOX 13819 MILWAUKEE, WI 53213

Visit Hal Leonard Online at
www.halleonard.com

ABOVE ALL

Words and Music by PAUL BALOCHE
and LENNY LeBLANC

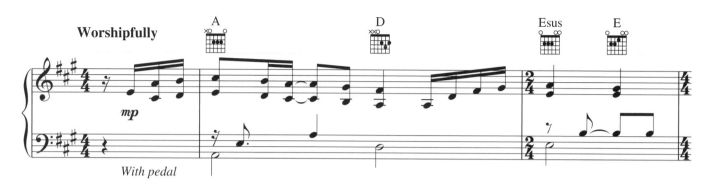

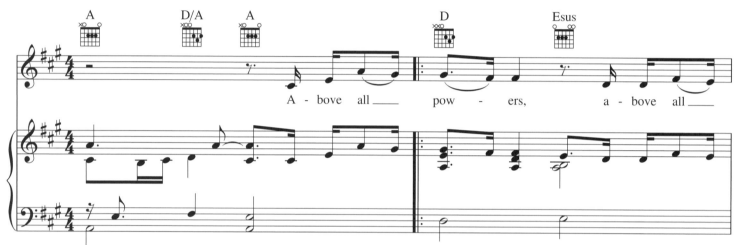

A - bove all ___ pow - ers, a - bove all ___

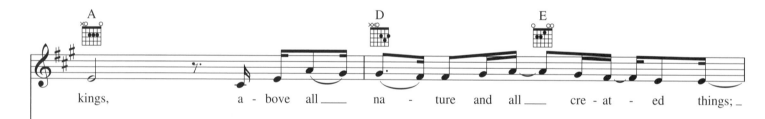

kings, a - bove all ___ na - ture and all ___ cre - at - ed things; ___

___ a - bove all wis - dom and all ___ the ways ___ of

man, _____ You were here __ be-fore __ the world __ be-gan. __

__ A - bove all ____ king - doms, a - bove all ____

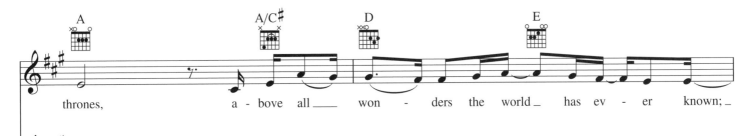

thrones, a - bove all ____ won - ders the world __ has ev - er known; __

__ a - bove all ____ wealth and treas - ures of ____ the

earth, _____ there's no way __ to meas - ure what __ You're

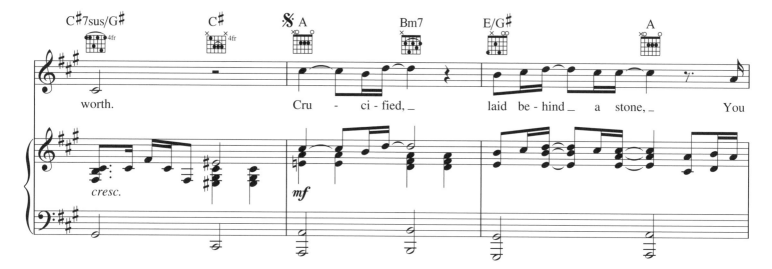

worth. Cru - ci - fied, __ laid be - hind __ a stone, __ You

lived __ to die __ re - ject - ed and __ a - lone. __ Like a rose __ tram - pled on __ the ground,

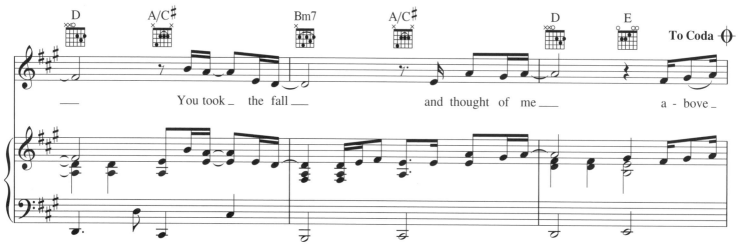

___ You took __ the fall ___ and thought of me ___ a - bove _

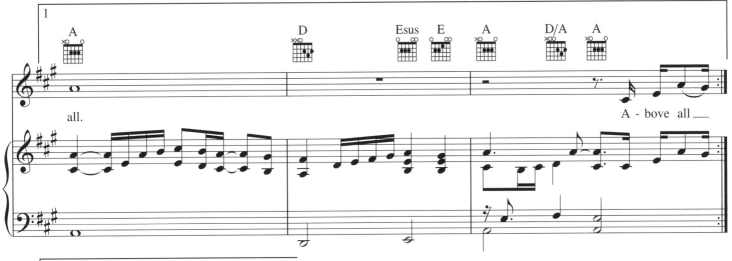

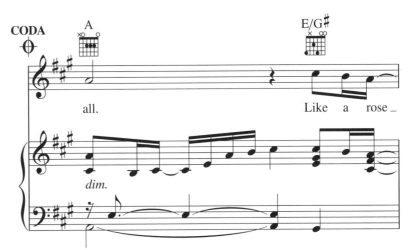

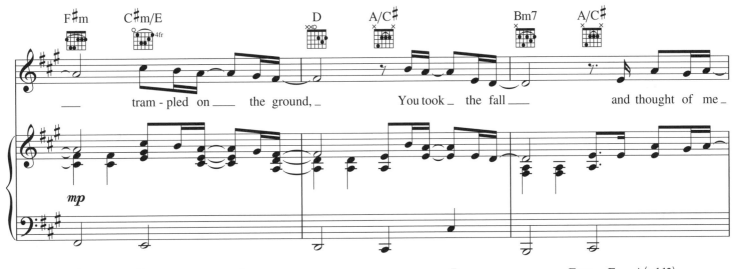

AT THE CROSS

Words and Music by REUBEN MORGAN
and DARLENE ZSCHECH

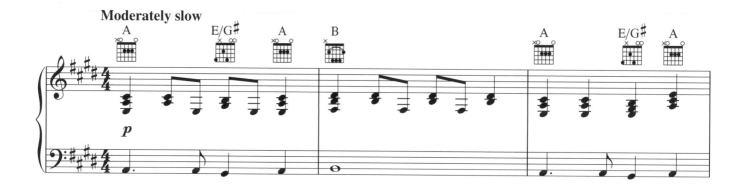

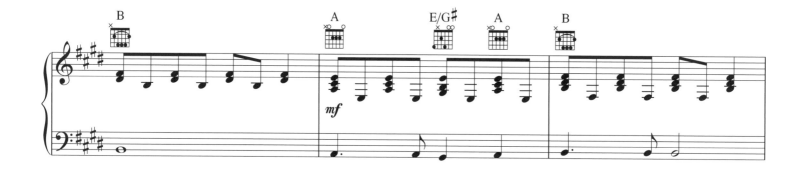

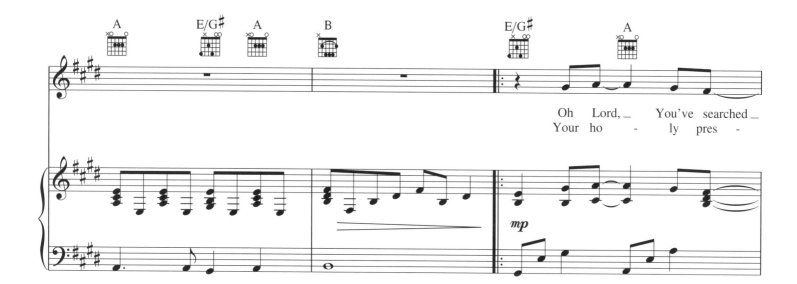

Oh Lord, __ You've searched __
Your ho - ly pres -

me, ___
- ence ___ You know ___ my way. ___
sur - round - ing me. ___

E - ven when ___ I fail ___ You, ___ I know ___ You
In ev - 'ry sea - son, ___ I know ___ You

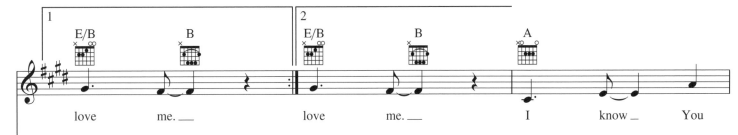

1
love me. ___

2
love me. ___ I know ___ You

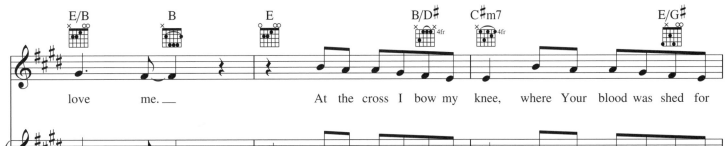

love me. ___ At the cross I bow my knee, where Your blood was shed for

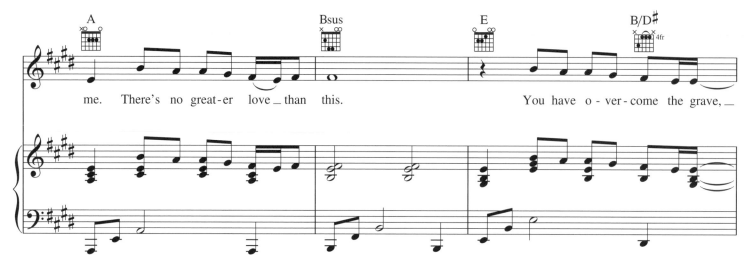

me. There's no great-er love __ than this. You have o-ver-come the grave, __

__ Your glo-ry fills the high-est place. What can sep-a-rate __ me now?

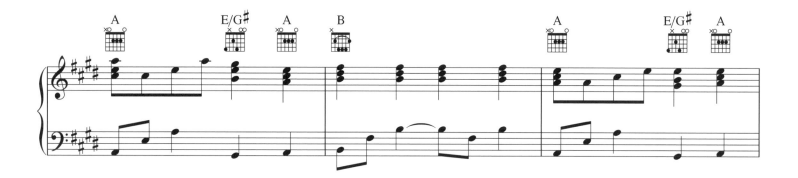

You go __ be-fore __ me, __

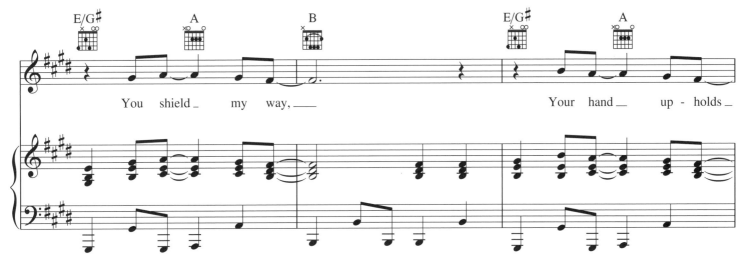

You shield __ my way, ___ Your hand __ up - holds __

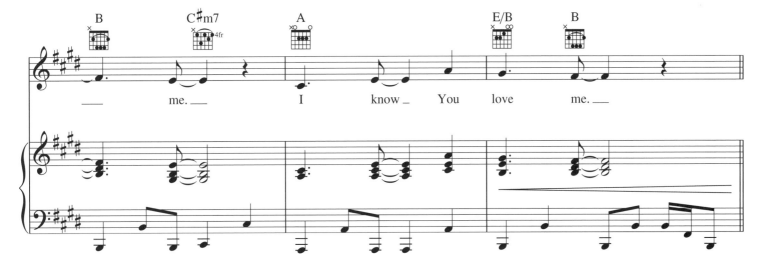

__ me. ___ I know __ You love me. ___

At the cross I bow my knee, where Your blood was shed for

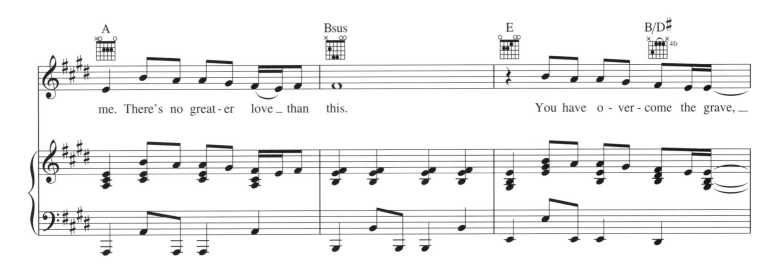

me. There's no great - er love __ than this. You have o - ver - come the grave, __

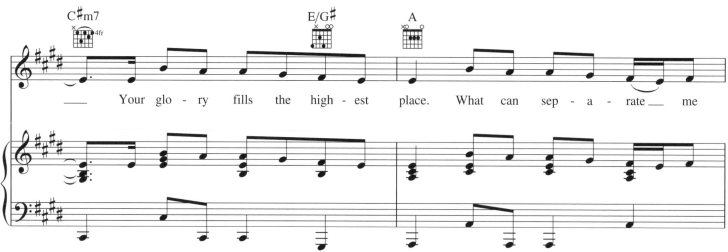

Your glo - ry fills the high - est place. What can sep - a - rate — me

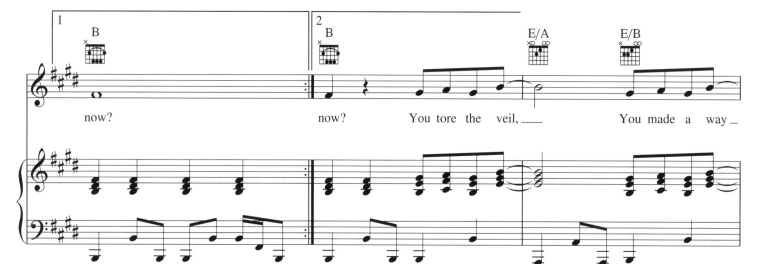

now? now? You tore the veil, — You made a way —

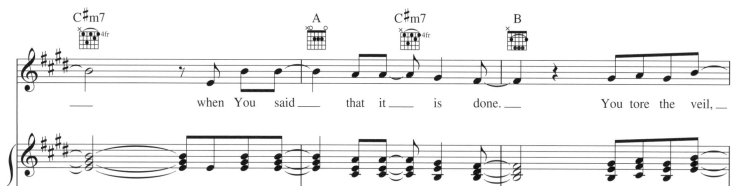

— when You said — that it — is done. — You tore the veil, —

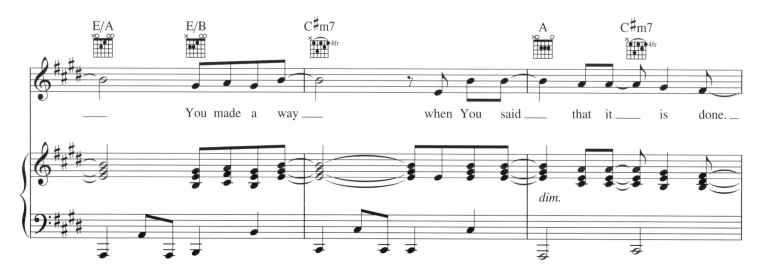

— You made a way — when You said — that it — is done. —

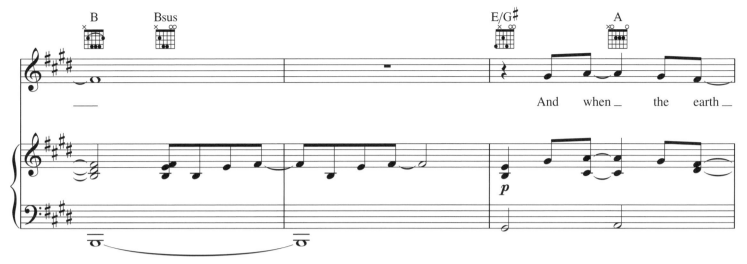

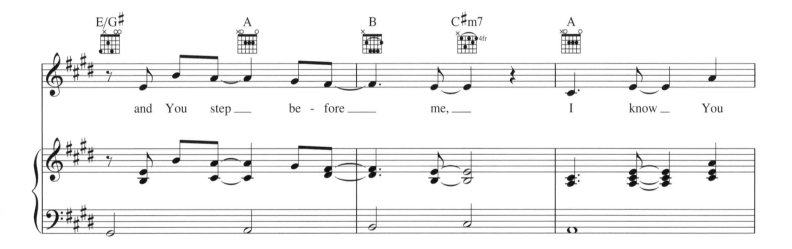

At the cross I bow my knee, where Your blood was shed for

me. There's no great-er love ___ than this.

You have o-ver-come the grave, ___ Your glo-ry fills the high-est

place. What can sep-a-rate me now? At the cross I bow my

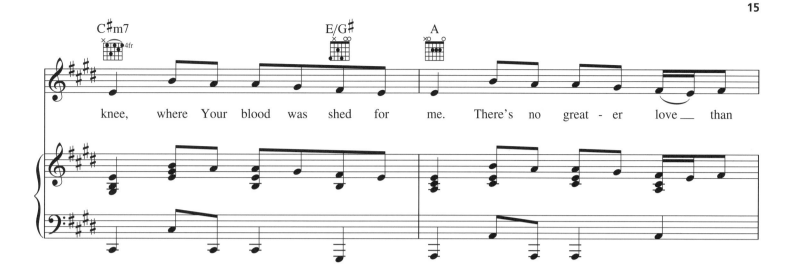

knee, where Your blood was shed for me. There's no great-er love ___ than

this. You have o-ver-come the grave, ___

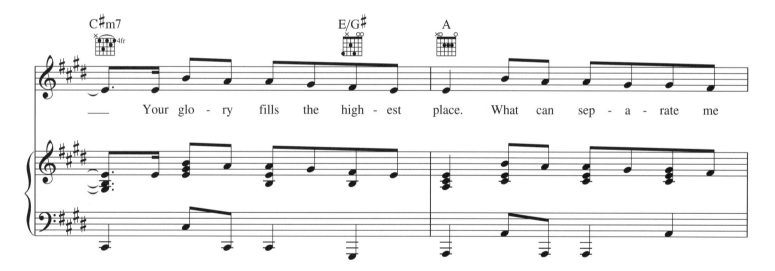

___ Your glo-ry fills the high-est place. What can sep-a-rate me

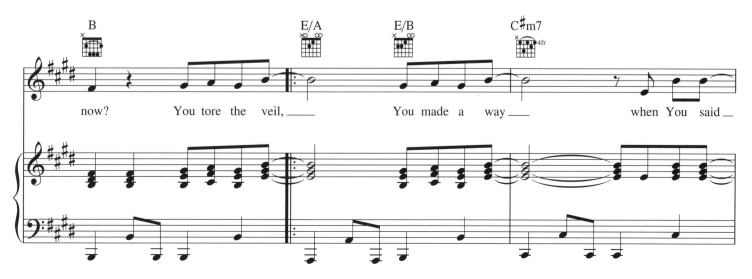

now? You tore the veil, ___ You made a way ___ when You said ___

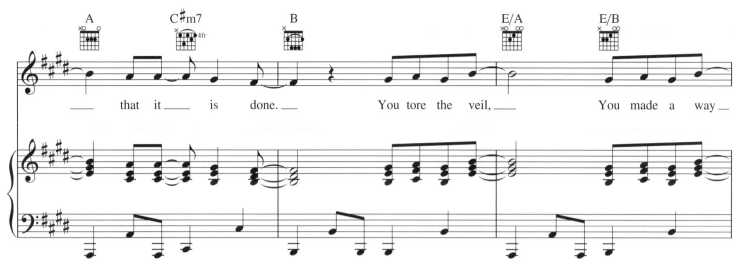

that it ___ is done. ___ You tore the veil, ___ You made a way ___

1
when You said ___ that it ___ is done. ___ You tore the veil, ___

2
when You said ___ that it ___ is done. ___

dim.

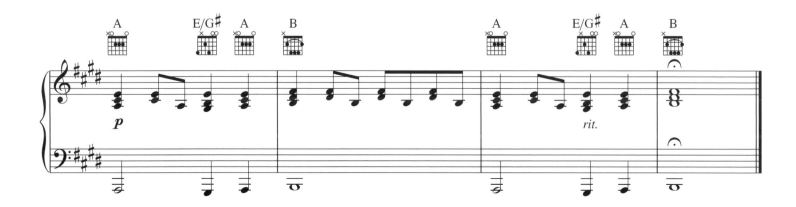

p

rit.

BROKEN AND BEAUTIFUL

Words and Music by BRIAN DOERKSEN
and JOSH FOX

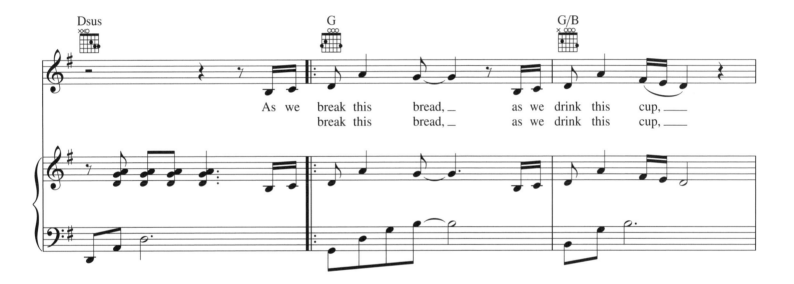

As we break this bread, _ as we drink this cup, ___
break this bread, _ as we drink this cup, ___

Lord, we re-mem-ber how You gave Your life _ on a
Lord, we re-mem-ber it was for my sin _ that Your

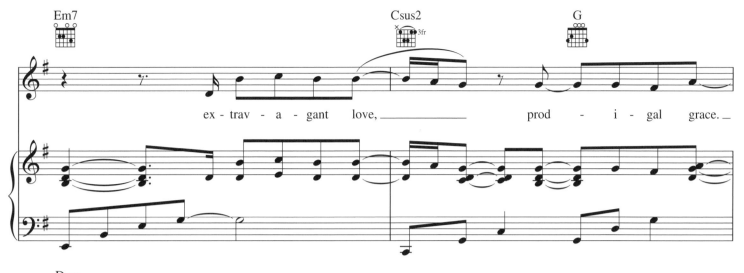

ex - trav - a - gant love,_____ prod - i - gal grace._

_ Bro - ken and beau - ti - ful,_ God's per - fect jus -

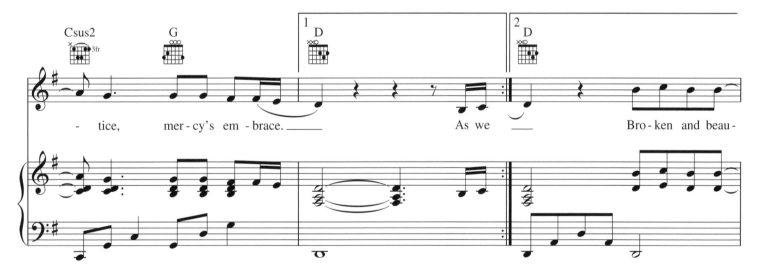

- tice, mer - cy's em - brace._ As we _ Bro - ken and beau -

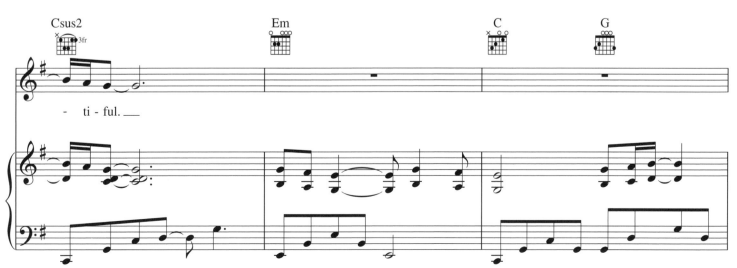

- ti - ful._

Bro - ken and beau - ti - ful. ____

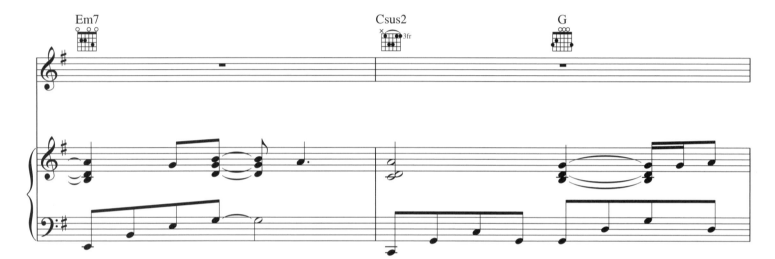

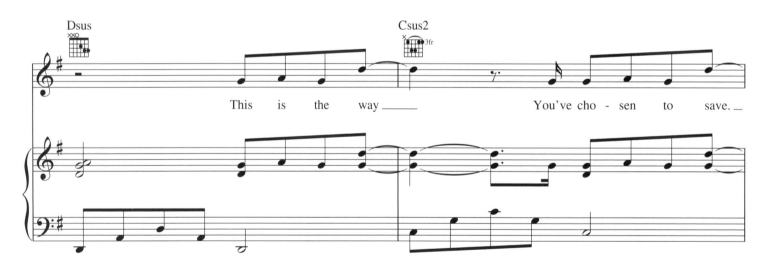

This is the way ____ You've cho - sen to save. __

__ This is the way ____ You make all ____ things new. __

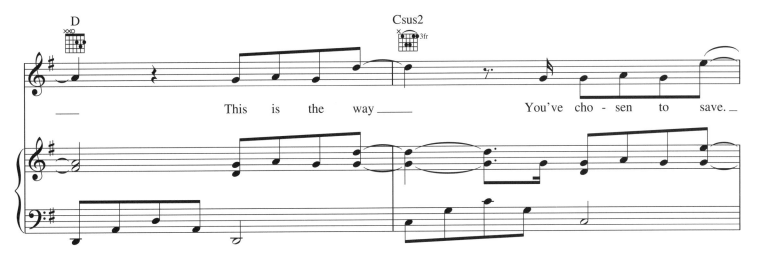

This is the way _____ You've cho - sen to save. _

_____ This is the way _____ You make all _____ things new. _____

_____ As we break this bread, _ as we drink this cup, _____

Lord, we re - mem - ber.

rit.

AT THE FOOT OF THE CROSS

Words and Music by
KATHRYN SCOTT

At the foot of the cross, ___ where grace ___ and suf-f'ring meet, ___
At the foot of the cross, ___ where I ___ am made _ com-plete, ___

(D.C.) *Instrumental*

You have shown me Your love ___ through _ the judg-
You have giv-en me life ___ through _ the death _

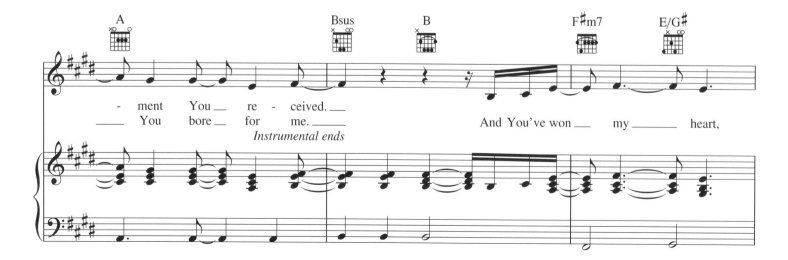

-ment You re-ceived. ___
___ You bore _ for me. ___

Instrumental ends

And You've won ___ my ___ heart,

yes, You've won __ my __ heart. Now I __ can

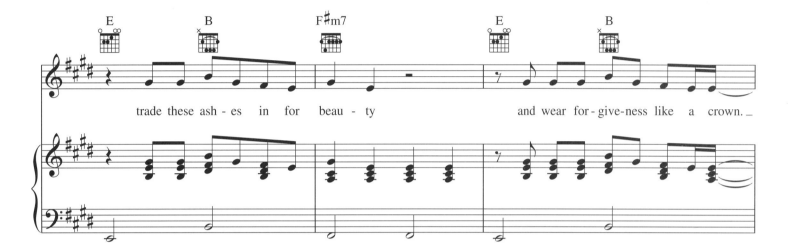

trade these ash - es in for beau - ty and wear for-give-ness like a crown. __

__ Com - ing to kiss the feet of mer - cy, I lay

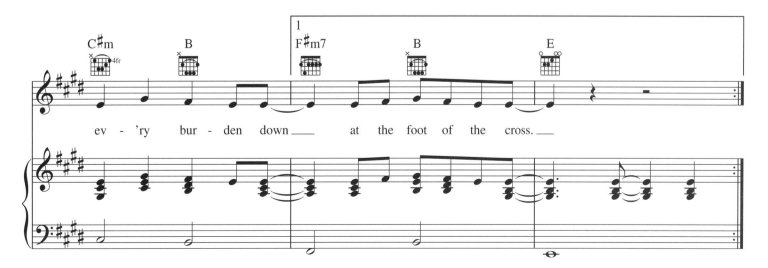

ev - 'ry bur - den down __ at the foot of the cross. __

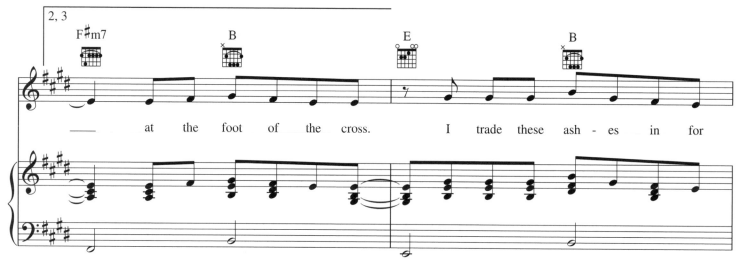

at the foot of the cross. I trade these ash - es in for

beau - ty and wear for - give - ness like a crown.

Com - ing to kiss the feet of mer - cy, I lay

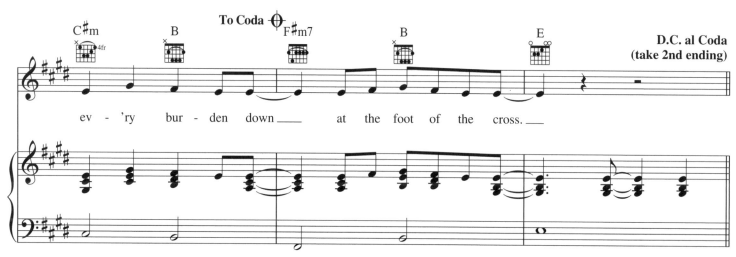

ev - 'ry bur - den down at the foot of the cross.

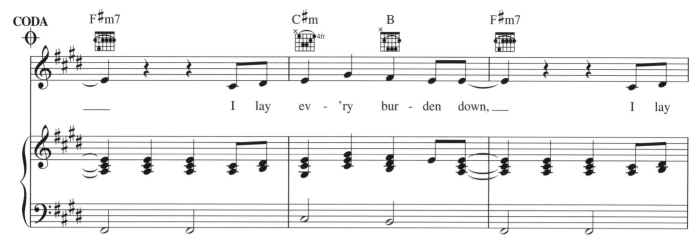

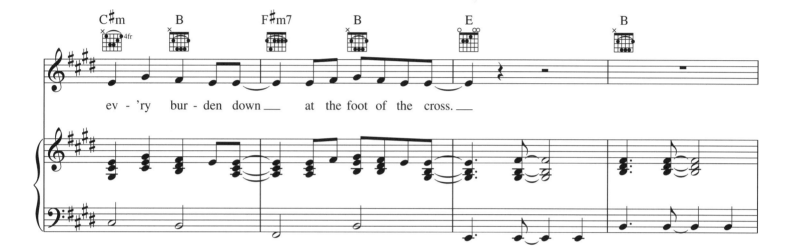

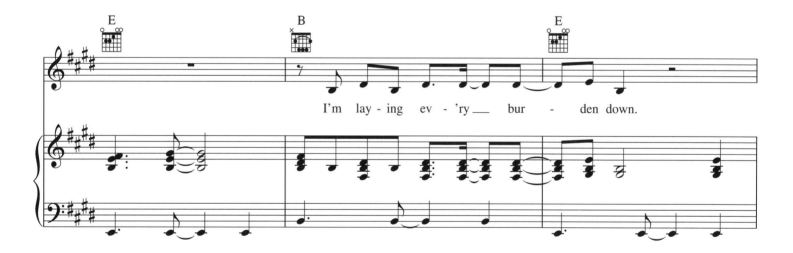

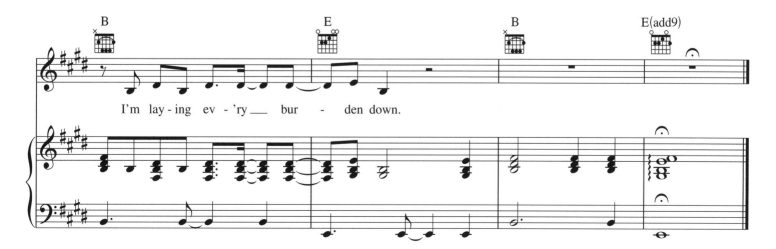

BY HIS WOUNDS

Words and Music by MAC POWELL
and DAVID NASSER

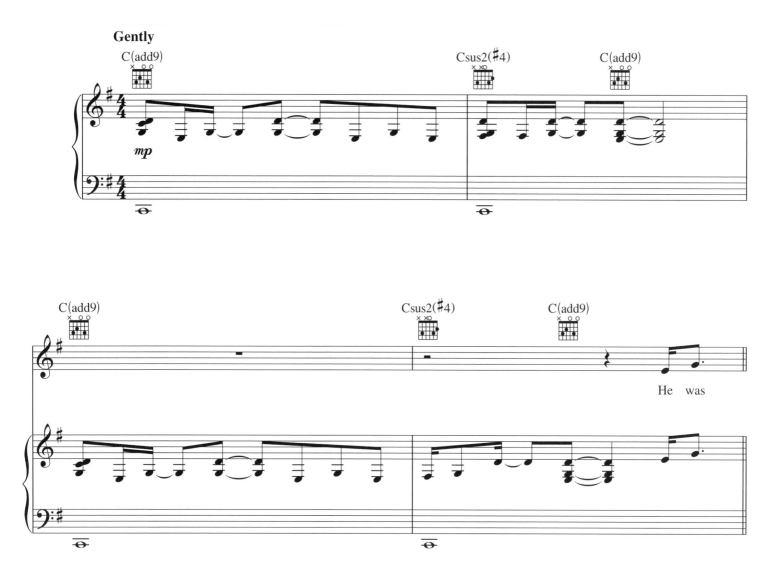

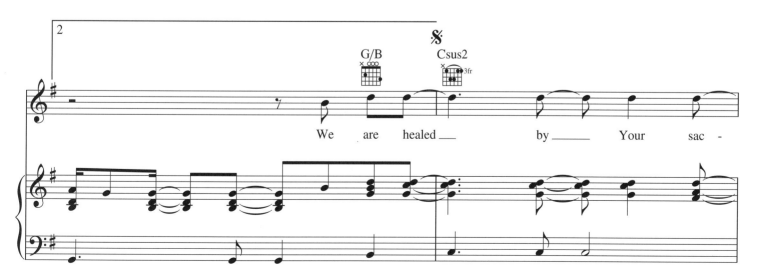

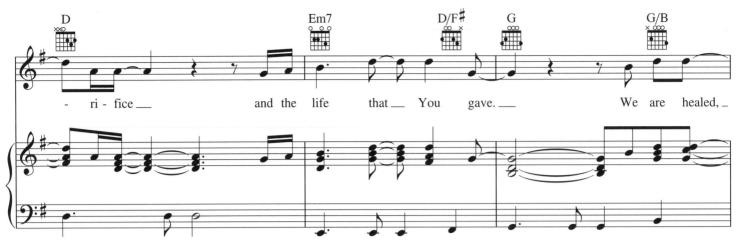

-ri - fice ___ and the life that ___ You gave. ___ We are healed, ___

___ for ___ You paid ___ the price. ___ By Your grace we ___ are saved, ___

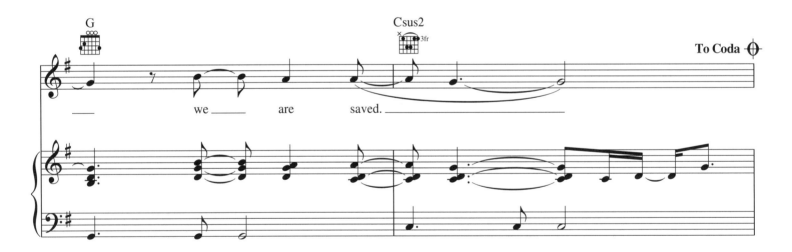

To Coda ⊕

we ___ are saved. _____

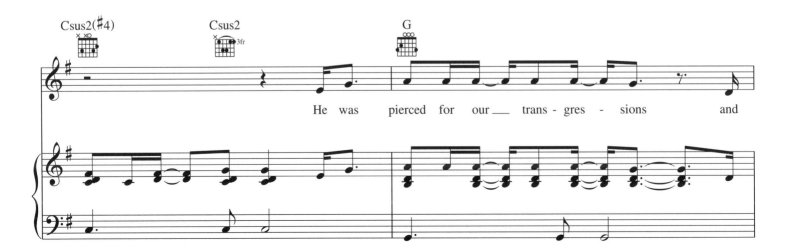

He was pierced for our ___ trans - gres - sions and

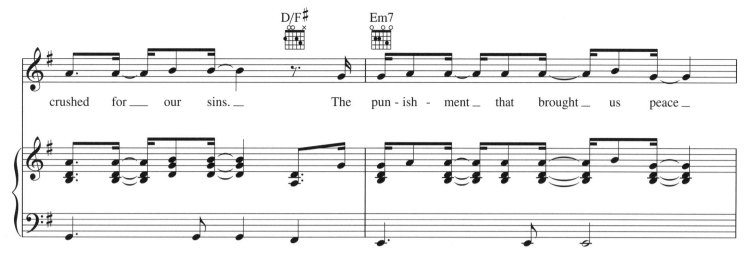

crushed for ___ our sins. ___ The pun - ish - ment ___ that brought ___ us peace ___

was up - on ___ Him. ___ And by His ___ wounds, ___

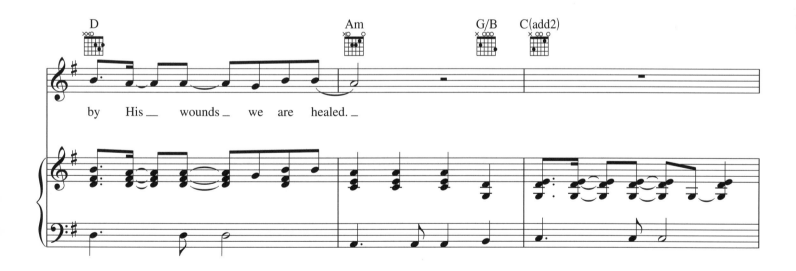

by His ___ wounds ___ we are healed. ___

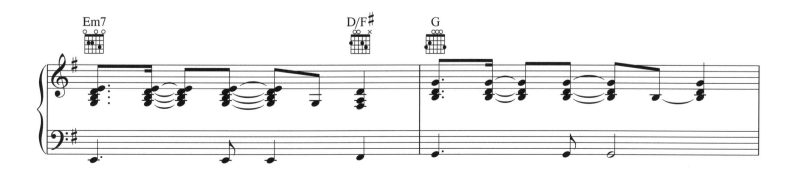

D.S. al Coda

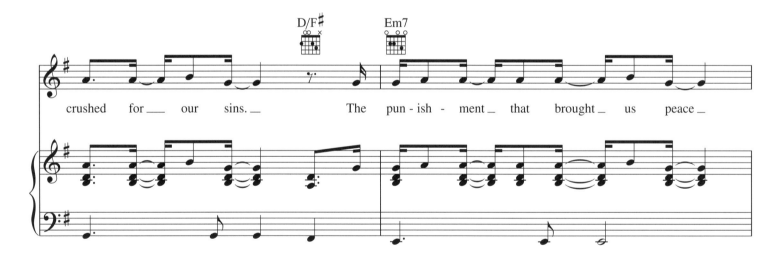

by His __ wounds __ we are healed. __

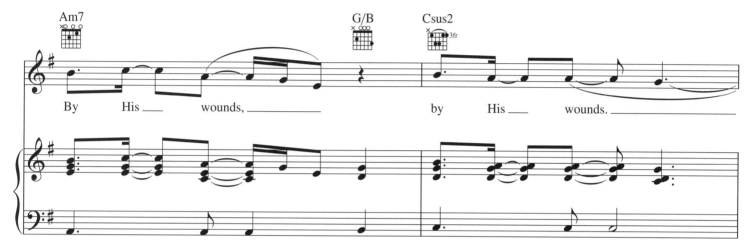

By His __ wounds, _____ by His __ wounds. _____

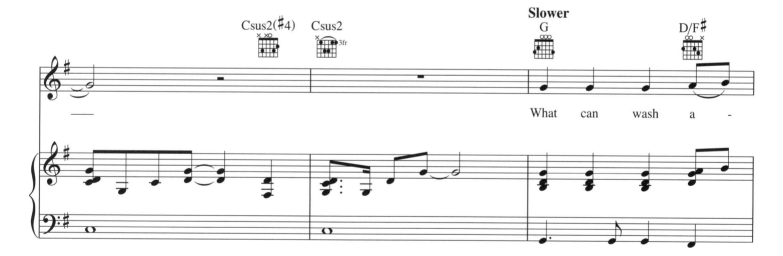

Slower

__ What can wash a -

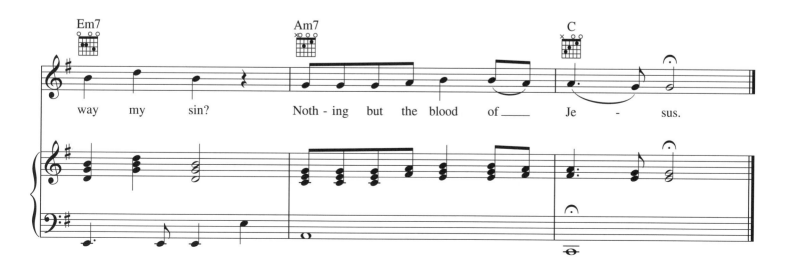

way my sin? Noth-ing but the blood of __ Je - sus.

FOR THE CROSS

Words and Music by MATT REDMAN
and BETH REDMAN

Moderately fast

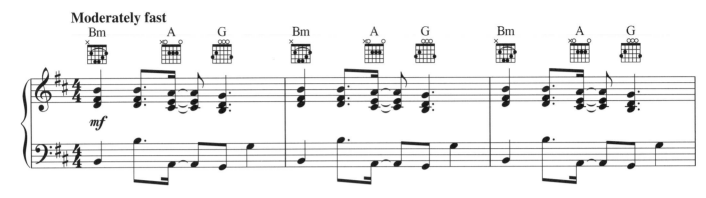

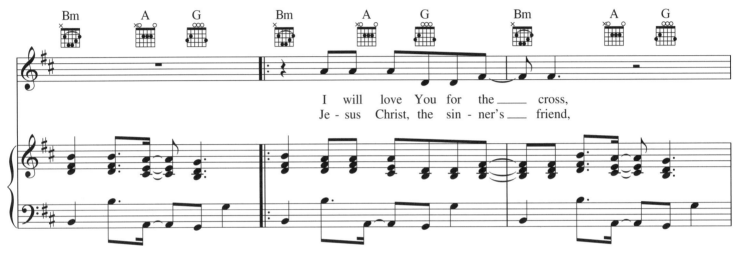

I will love You for the _____ cross,
Je - sus Christ, the sin - ner's _____ friend,

and I will love You for the _____ cost.
does this kind - ness know no _____ bounds?

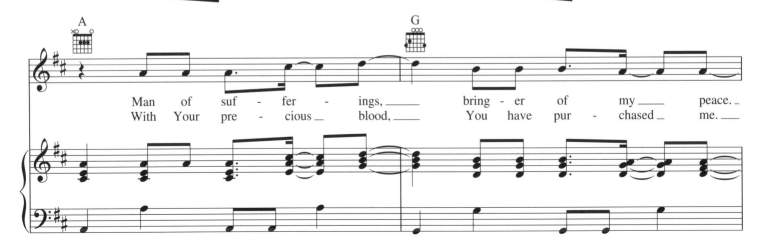

Man of suf - fer - ings, _____ bring - er of my _____ peace.
With Your pre - cious _____ blood, _____ You have pur - chased _____ me. _____

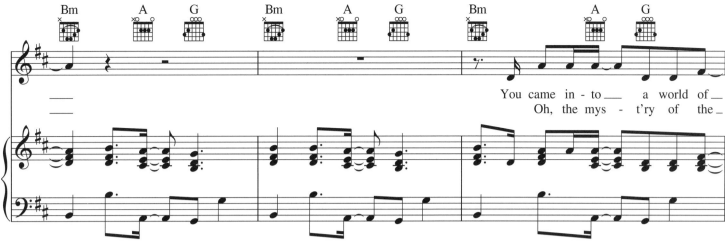

You came in - to ___ a world of ___
Oh, the mys - t'ry of the ___

___ shame, ___ and paid the price ___ we could not ___
___ cross. ___ You were pun - ished, You were ___

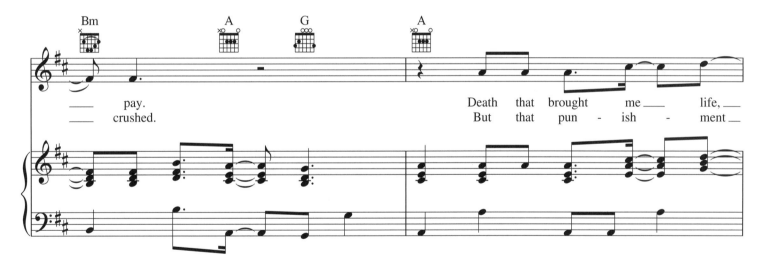

___ pay. ___ Death that brought me ___ life, ___
___ crushed. ___ But that pun - ish - ment ___

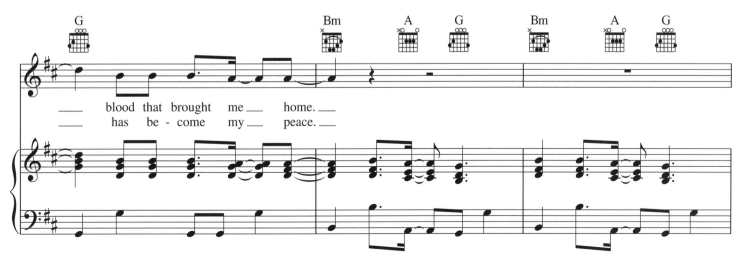

___ blood that brought me ___ home. ___
___ has be - come my ___ peace. ___

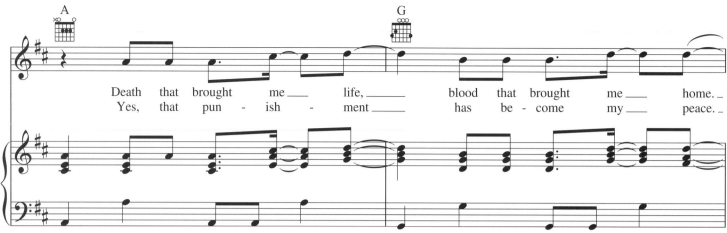

Death that brought me ___ life, ___ blood that brought me ___ home. ___
Yes, that pun - ish - ment ___ has be - come my ___ peace. ___

And ___ I love ___ You for ___ the cross. ___

I'm o - ver - whelmed by the mys - ter - y. ___ I love ___

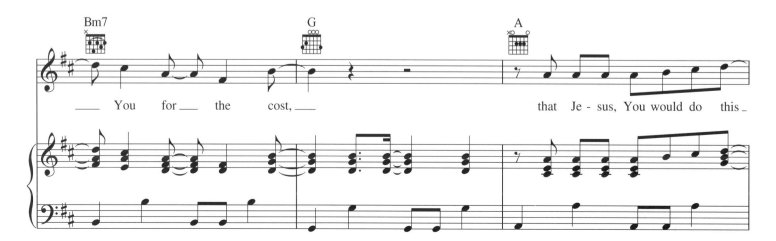

___ You for ___ the cost, ___ that Je - sus, You would do this ___

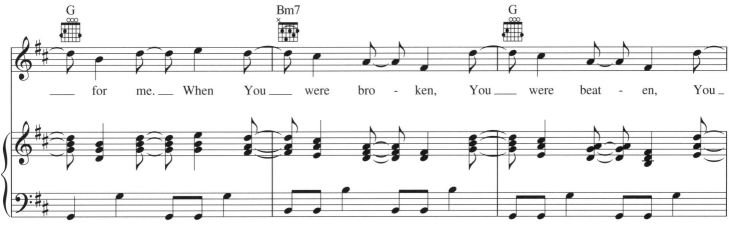

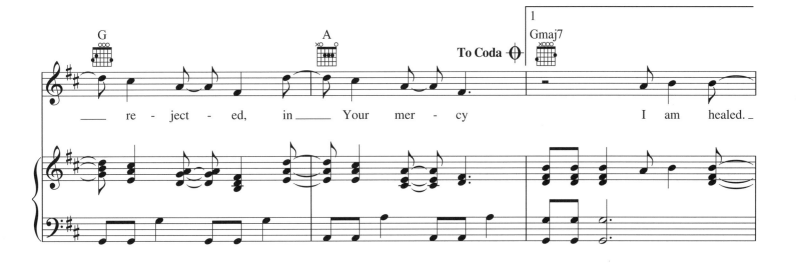

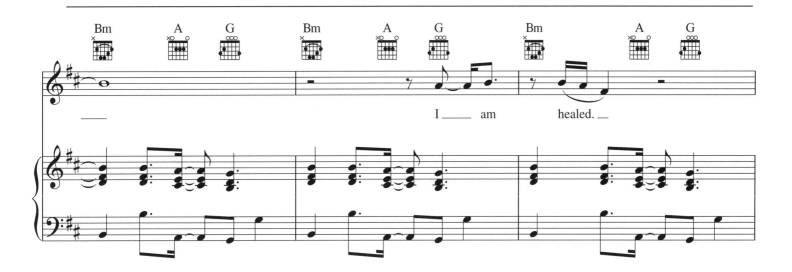

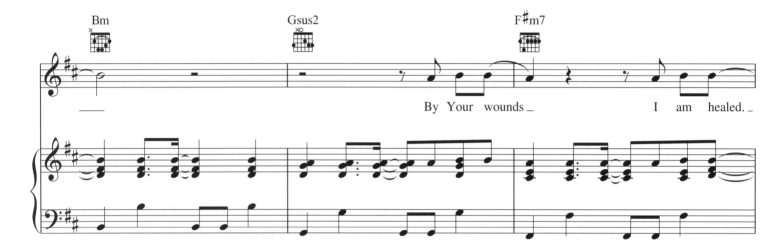

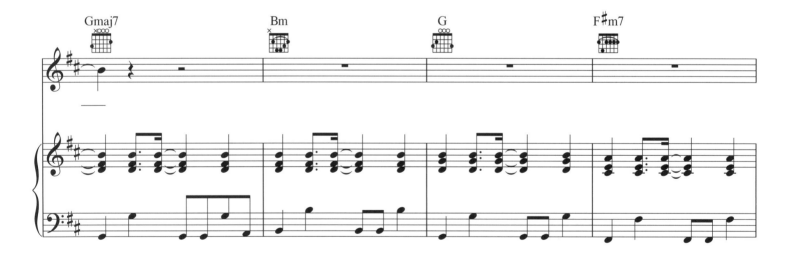

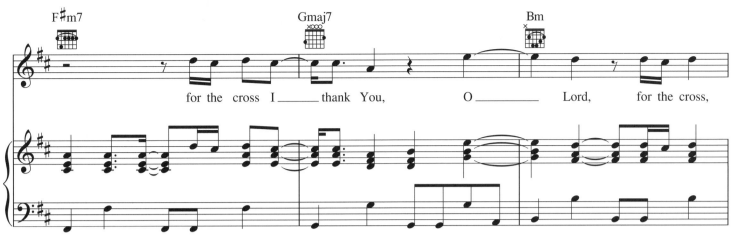

for the cross I _____ thank You, O _____ Lord, for the cross,

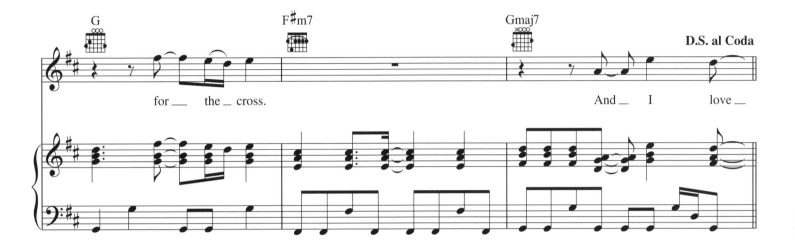

D.S. al Coda

for _ the _ cross. And _ I love _

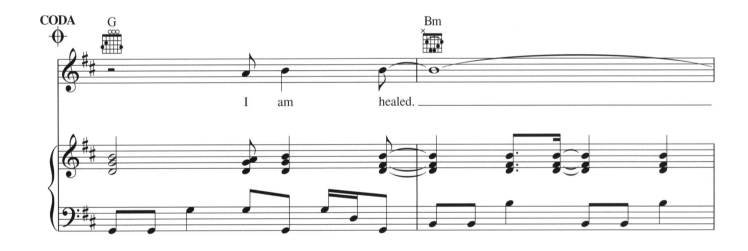

CODA

I am healed. _____

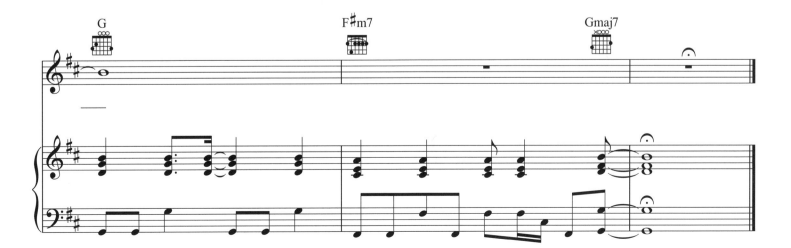

GRACE FLOWS DOWN

Words and Music by LOUIE GIGLIO,
DAVID BELL and ROD PADGETT

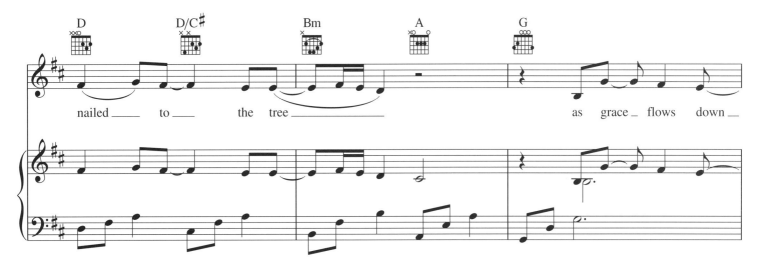

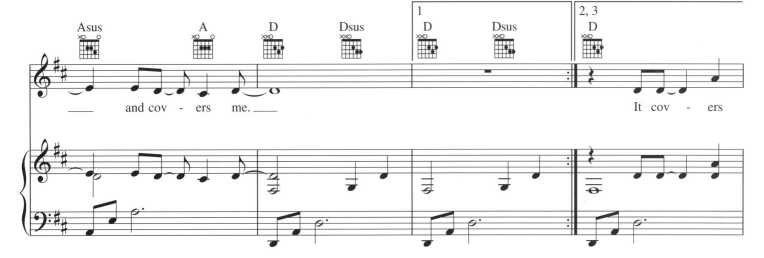

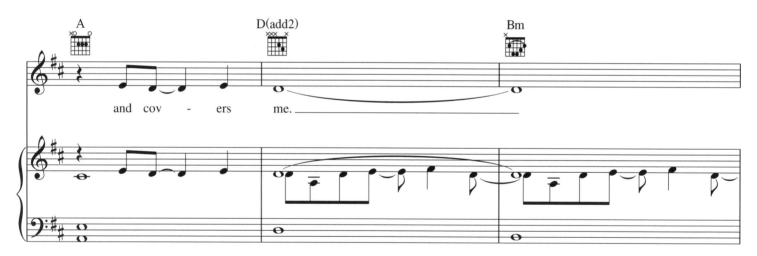

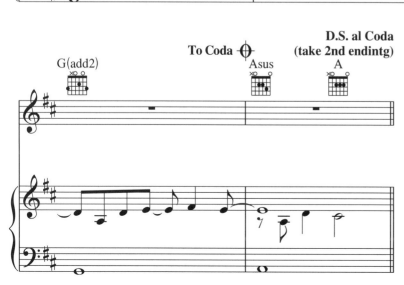

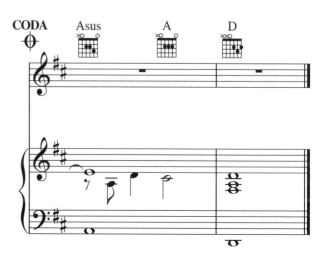

I COME TO THE CROSS

Words and Music by BILL BATSTONE
and BOB SOMMA

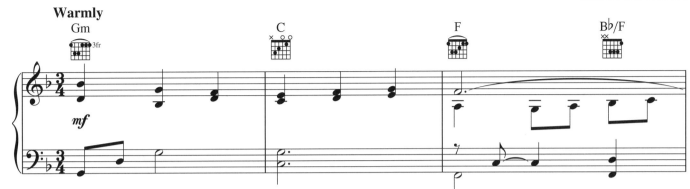

I come to the cross seek-ing mer-cy and

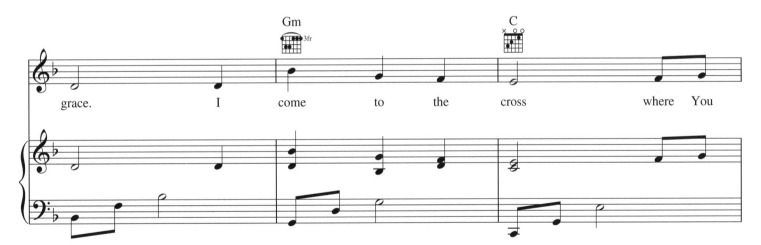

grace. I come to the cross where You

died in my ___ place. Out of my

weak - ness and in - to Your strength,

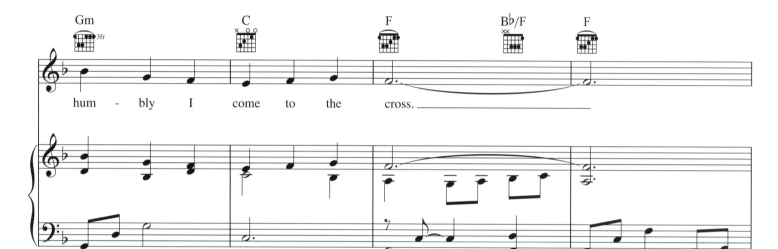

hum - bly I come to the cross. _____

Your arms are o - pen, You call me by

name. You wel - come _____ this child that was

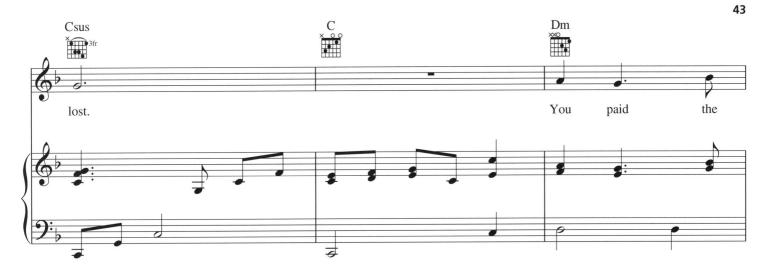

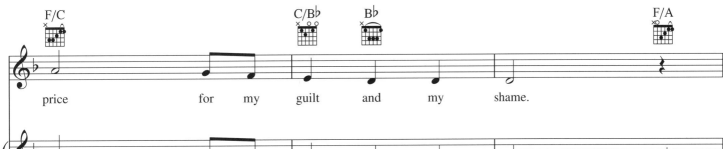

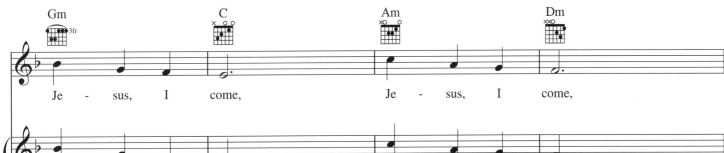

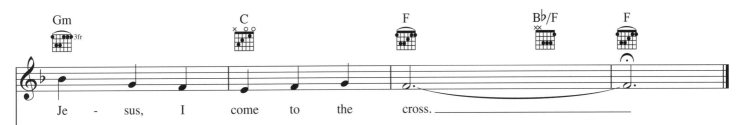

HOW DEEP THE FATHER'S LOVE FOR US

Words and Music by
STUART TOWNEND

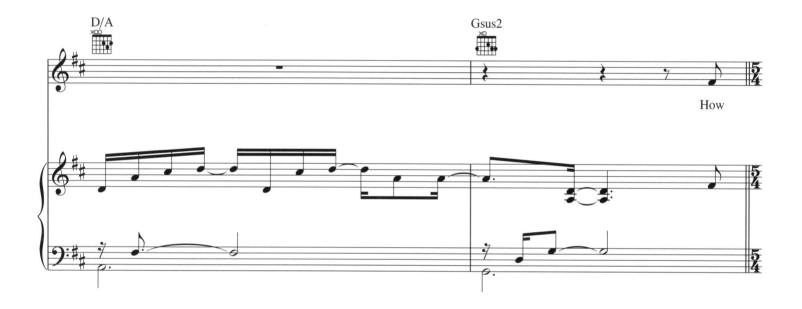

deep the Fa - ther's love for us; how vast be - yond all meas - ure that
hold the man up - on a cross, my sin up - on His shoul - ders. A -
will not boast in an - y - thing, no gifts, no pow'r, no wis - dom, but

He should give His on-ly Son   to make a wretch His treas-ure.   How
shamed, I hear my mock-ing voice   call out a-mong the scoff-ers.   It
I will boast in Je-sus Christ,   His death and res-ur-rec-tion.   Why

great the pain of sear-ing loss.   The Fa-ther turns His face a-way   as
was my sin that held Him there   un-til it was ac-com-plished.   His
should I gain from His re-ward?   I can-not give an an-swer,   but

wounds which mar the Cho-sen One   bring man-y sons to glo-
dy-ing breath has brought me life.   I know that it is fin-
this I know with all my heart: His wounds have paid my ran-

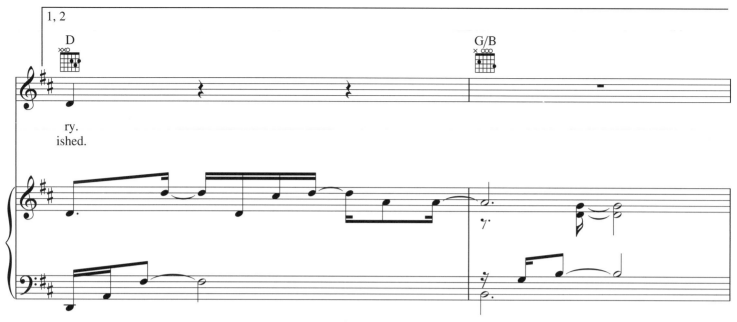

ry.
ished.

Be -
I

som. Why should I gain from His re - ward? I

can - not give an an - swer, but this I know with all my heart: His

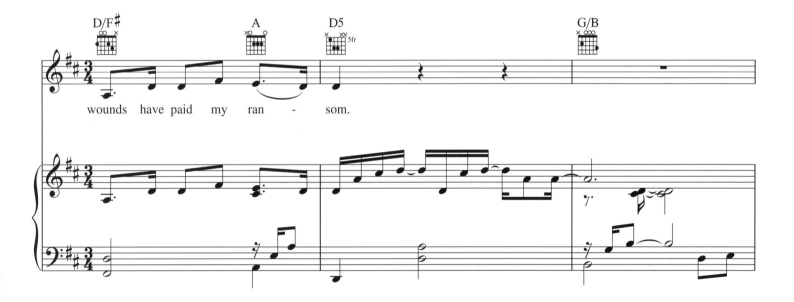

wounds have paid my ran - som.

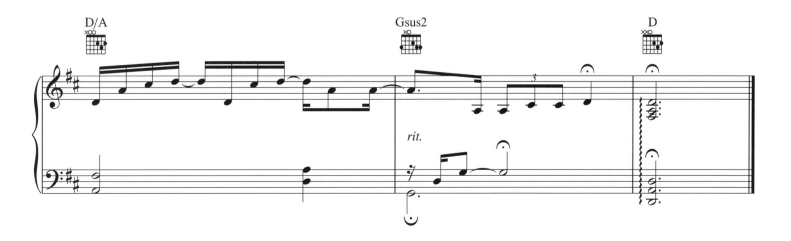

I CLING TO THE CROSS

Words and Music by PAUL BALOCHE
and MATT REDMAN

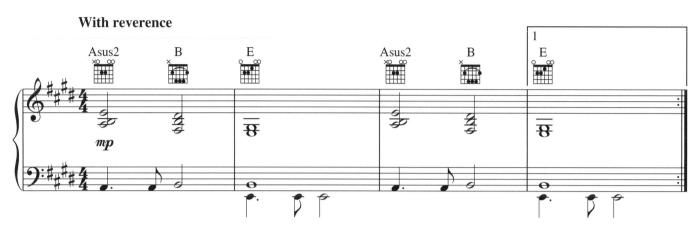

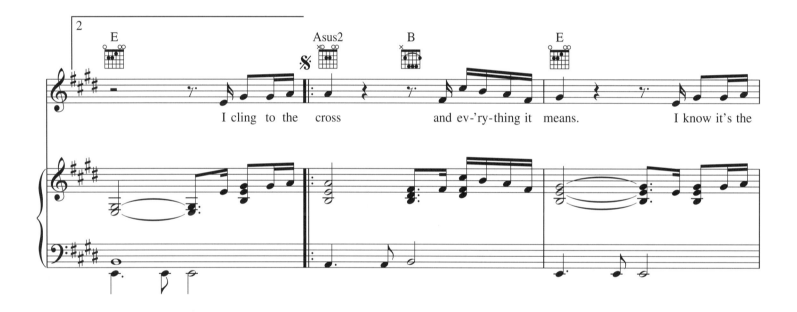

I cling to the cross and ev-'ry-thing it means. I know it's the

on-ly hope there is for sav-ing me. For with-out Your great mer-cy, I would

be for-ev-er lost, ___ so with a thank-ful heart ___ I come, ___

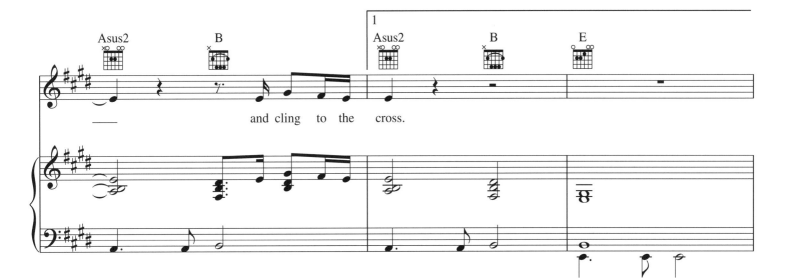

and cling to the cross.

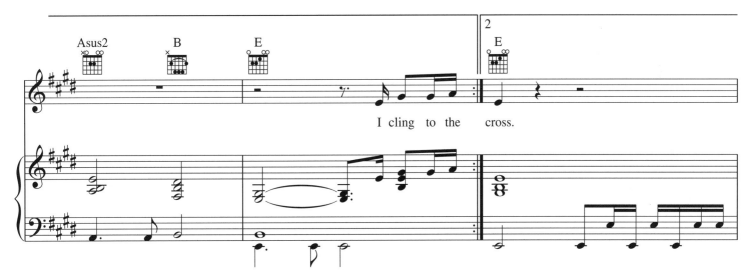

I cling to the cross.

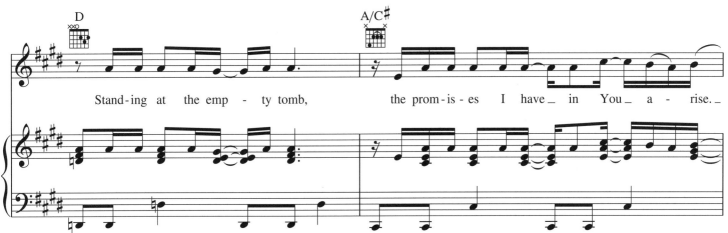

Stand-ing at the emp-ty tomb, the prom-is-es I have ___ in You a - rise. ___

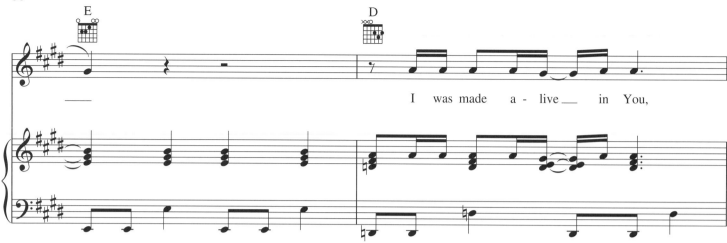

I was made a-live __ in You,

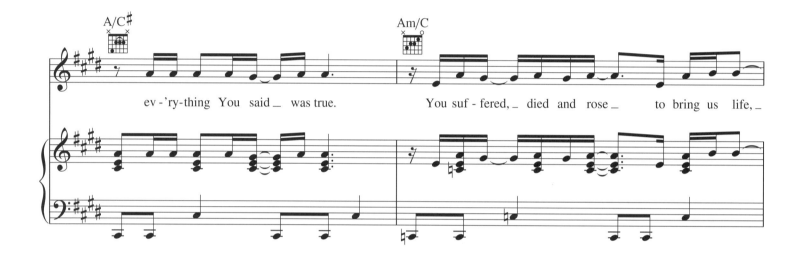

ev-'ry-thing You said __ was true. You suf-fered, __ died and rose __ to bring us life, __

bring us life. __ I cling to the

D.S. al Coda

__ Je-sus, I come. __ With a thank-ful heart __ I come, __ with a

thank-ful heart __ I come, __ and cling to the cross.

The world be - hind me, the cross be - fore me. The world be -

hind me, the cross be - fore me. The world be - hind me, the cross be -

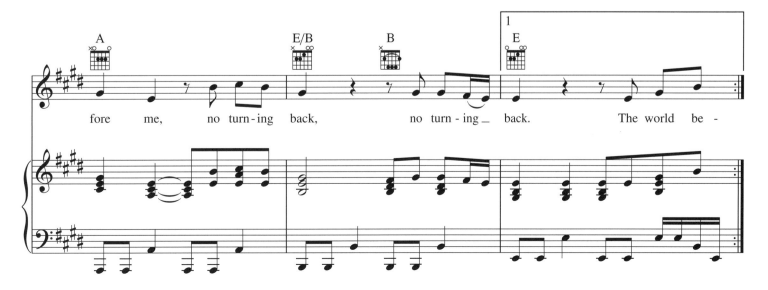

fore me, no turn-ing back, no turn-ing __ back. The world be -

back. The world be-hind me, the cross be-

fore me. The world be-hind me, the cross be-fore me. The world be-

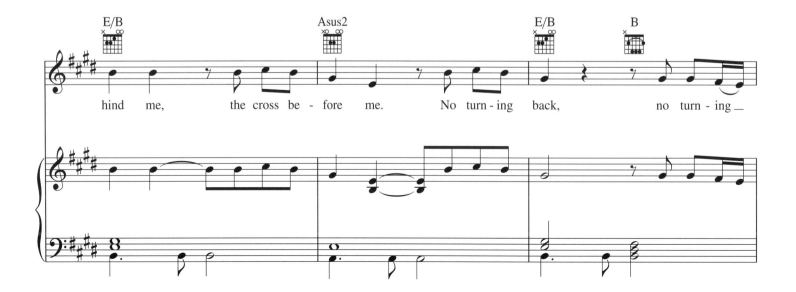

hind me, the cross be-fore me. No turn-ing back, no turn-ing

back, no turn - ing __ back.

I cling to the cross and ev - 'ry - thing it means, Lord. I cling to the

cross, there's no oth - er hope for me, God. I cling to the cross.

IN CHRIST ALONE

Words and Music by KEITH GETTY
and STUART TOWNEND

Moderately, with conviction

In Christ a - lone my hope is found; He is my
lone, who took on flesh, full - ness of
ground His bod - y lay, Light of the
life, no fear in death; this is the

light, my strength, my song. This cor - ner - stone, this sol - id
God in help - less Babe! This gift of love and right - eous -
world by dark - ness slain. Then burst - ing forth in glo - rious
pow'r of Christ in me. From life's first cry to fi - nal

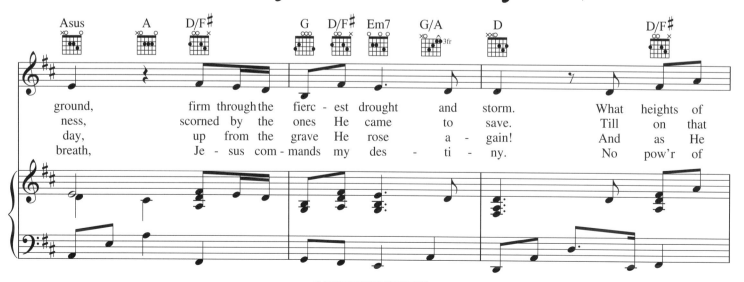

ground, firm through the fierc - est drought and storm. What heights of
ness, scorned by the ones He came to save. Till on that
day, up from the grave He rose a - gain! And as He
breath, Je - sus com - mands my des - ti - ny. No pow'r of

JESUS LORD OF HEAVEN

Words and Music by
PHIL WICKHAM

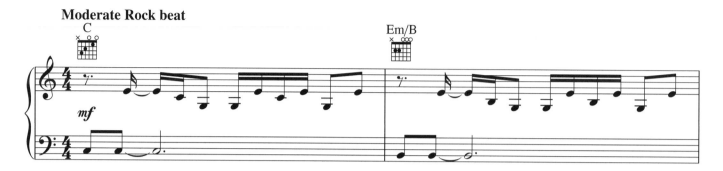

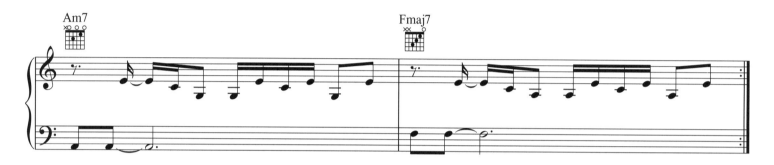

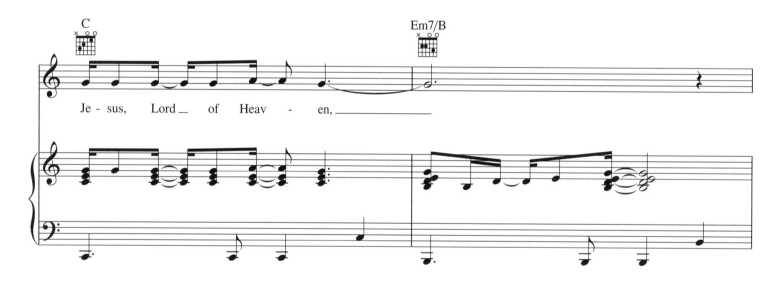

Je-sus, Lord__ of Heav__ en,_____

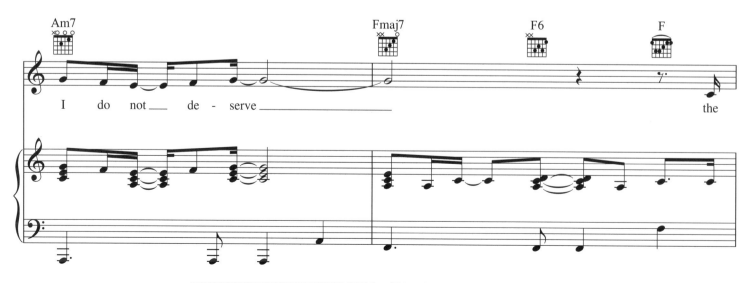

I do not__ de-serve _____ the

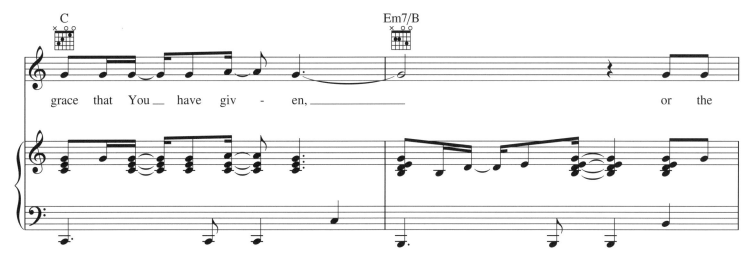

grace that You_ have giv - en, _____ or the

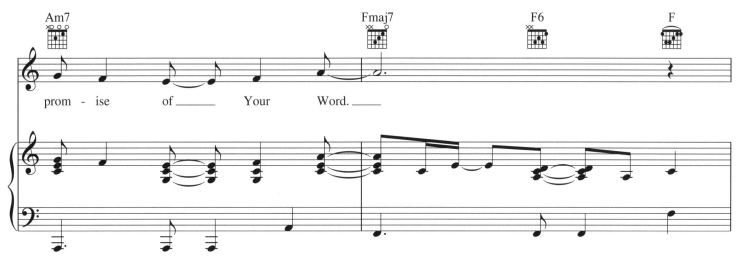

prom - ise of _____ Your Word. ____

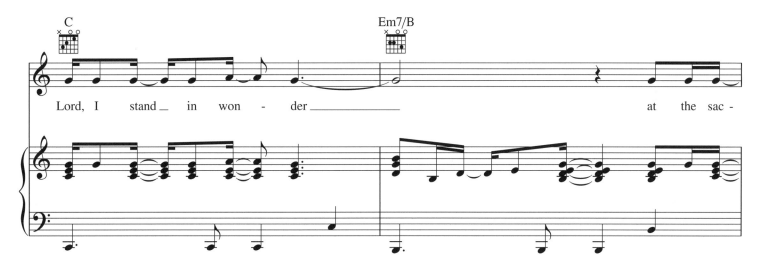

Lord, I stand_ in won - der _____ at the sac -

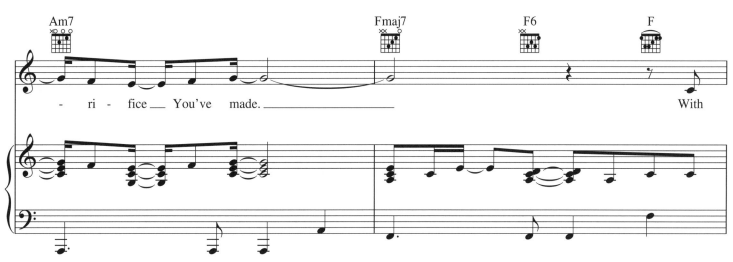

- ri - fice_ You've made. _____ With

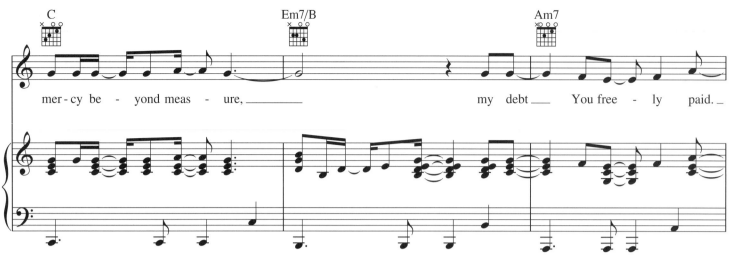

mer - cy be - yond meas - ure, _____ my debt ___ You free - ly paid. __

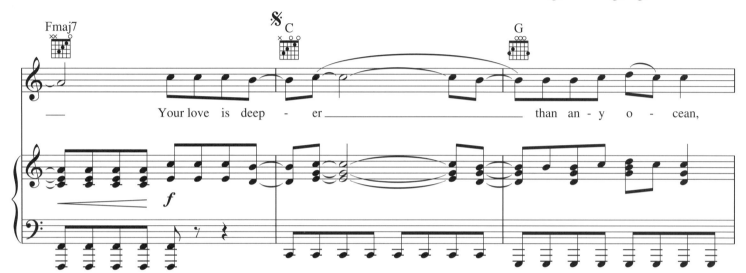

___ Your love is deep - er _____ than an - y o - cean,

high - er than the heav - ens, reach - es _____

To Coda ⊕

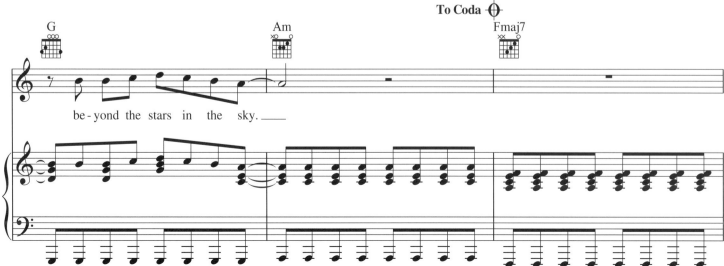

be - yond the stars in the sky. ___

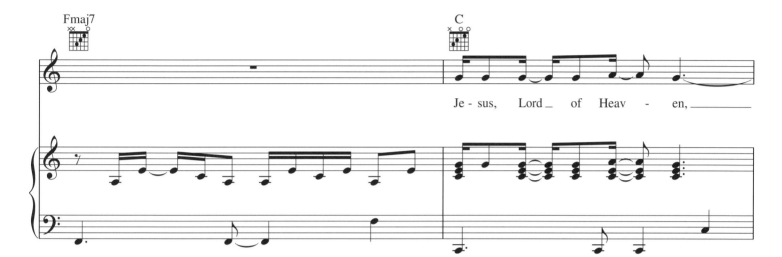

Je - sus, Lord __ of Heav __ - en, _____

__ I do not __ de - serve _____

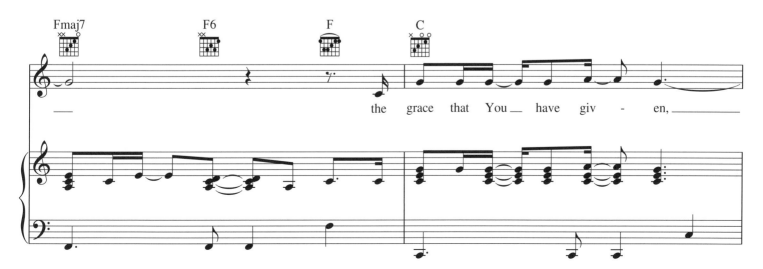

__ the grace that You __ have giv - en, _____

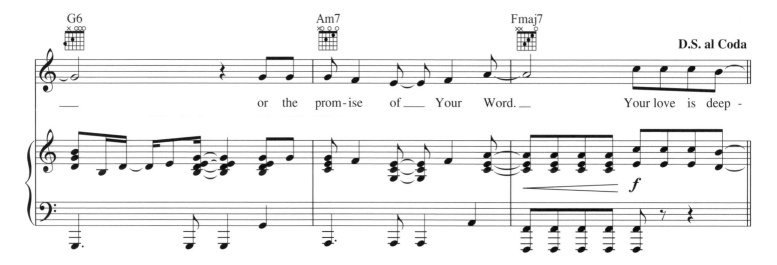

or the prom-ise of ___ Your Word. ___ Your love is deep -

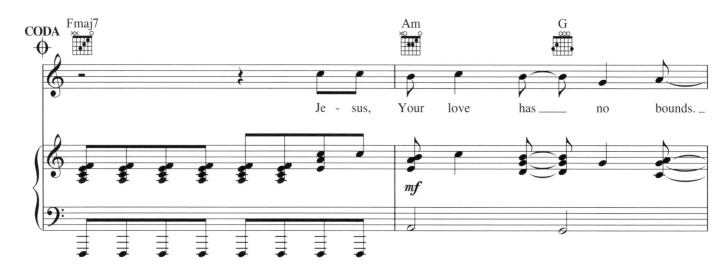

Je - sus, Your love has ___ no bounds. ___

Je - sus, Your love has ___ no bounds. ___ Je - sus,

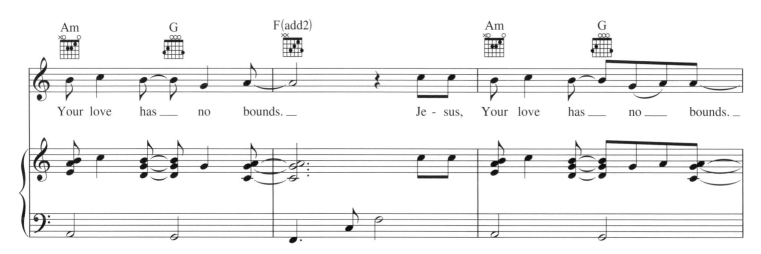

Your love has ___ no bounds. ___ Je - sus, Your love has ___ no ___ bounds. ___

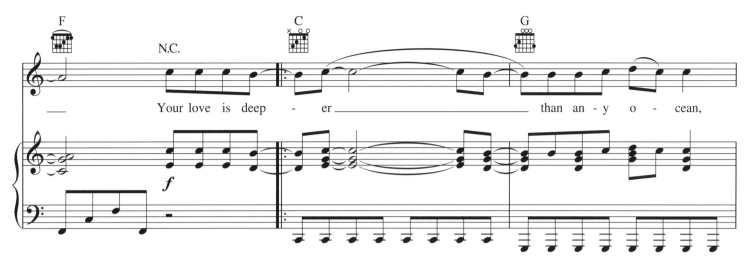

Your love is deep - er _____ than an - y o - cean,

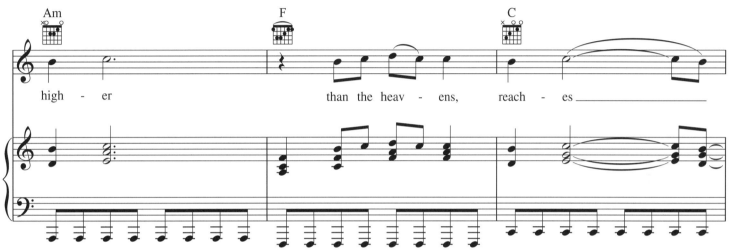

high - er _____ than the heav - ens, reach - es _____

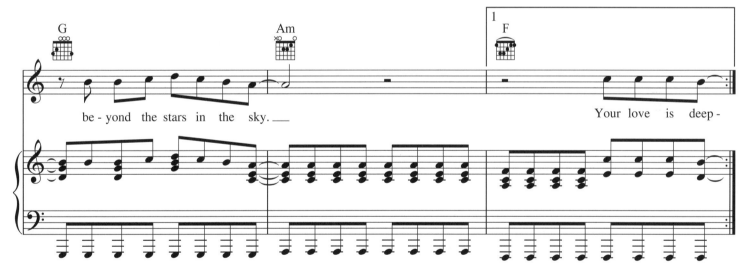

be - yond the stars in the sky. ___ Your love is deep -

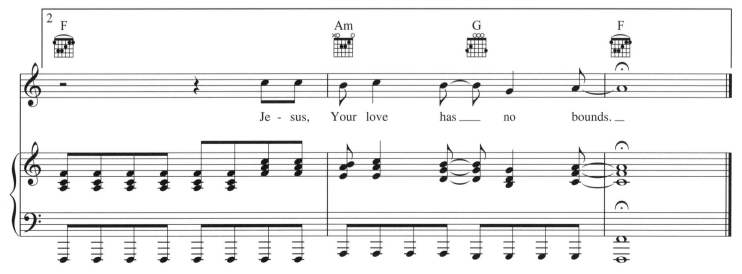

Je - sus, Your love has ___ no bounds. ___

JESUS MESSIAH

Words and Music by CHRIS TOMLIN,
JESSE REEVES, DANIEL CARSON
and ED CASH

With praise

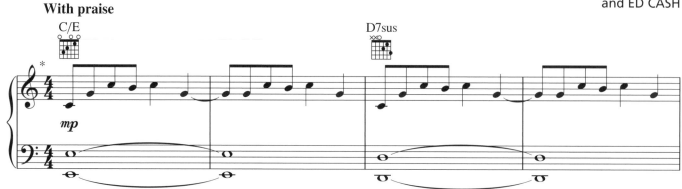

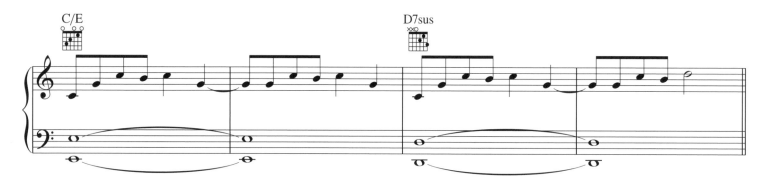

He be-came __ sin __ who knew no __ sin, __ that we might be-come __ His __

__ right-eous-ness. He hum-bled Him-self __ and car-ried the __ cross. __

Recorded a half step lower.

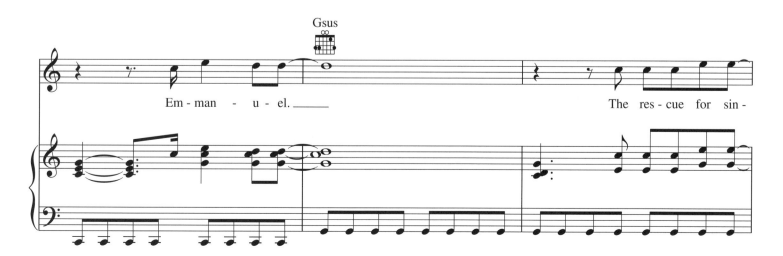

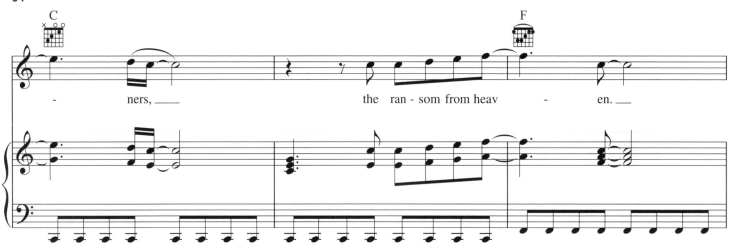

- ners, _____ the ran - som from heav - en. __

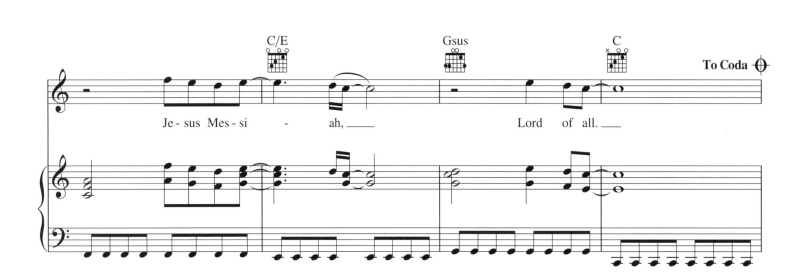

Je - sus Mes - si - ah, _____ Lord of all. ___

To Coda ⊕

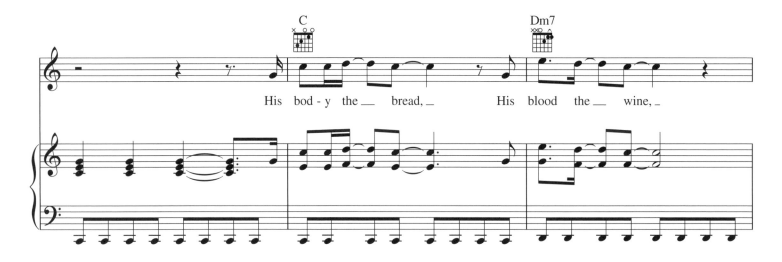

His bod - y the __ bread, _ His blood the __ wine, _

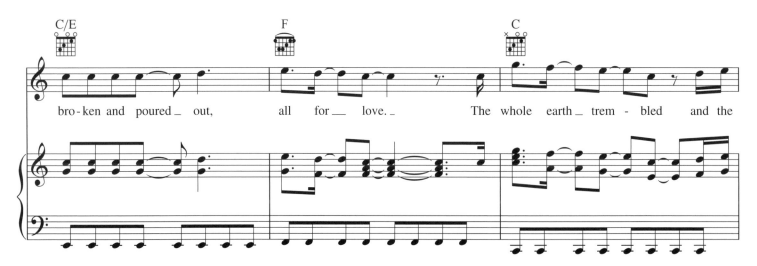

bro - ken and poured _ out, all for _ love. _ The whole earth _ trem - bled and the

Dm7   C/G   F

veil was __ torn. _____ Love so a - maz - ing, __

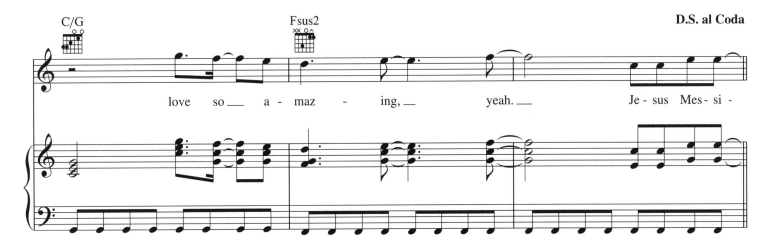

C/G   Fsus2   **D.S. al Coda**

love so __ a - maz - ing, __ yeah. __ Je - sus Mes - si -

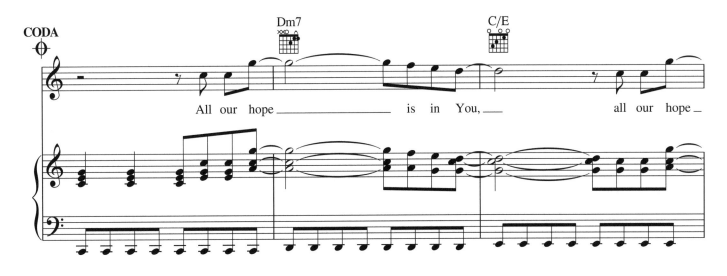

CODA   Dm7   C/E

All our hope _____ is in You, __ all our hope __

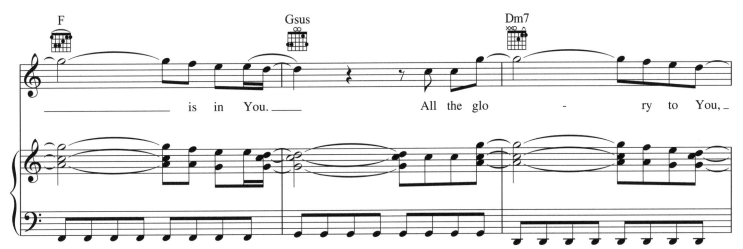

F   Gsus   Dm7

_____ is in You. __ All the glo - ry to You, __

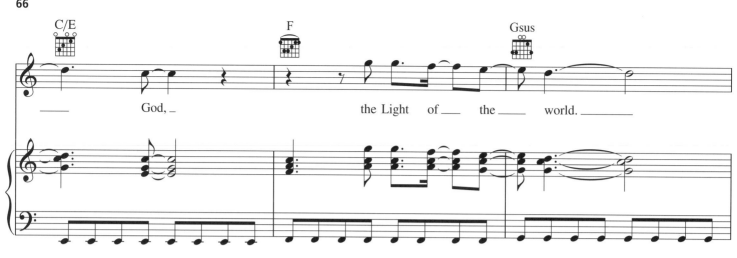

God, _ the Light of _ the _ world. _____

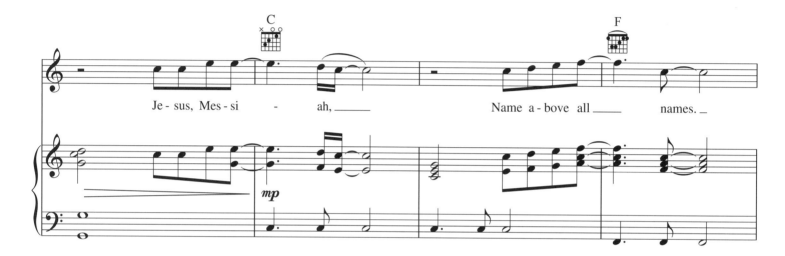

Je - sus, Mes - si - ah, _____ Name a - bove all _____ names. _

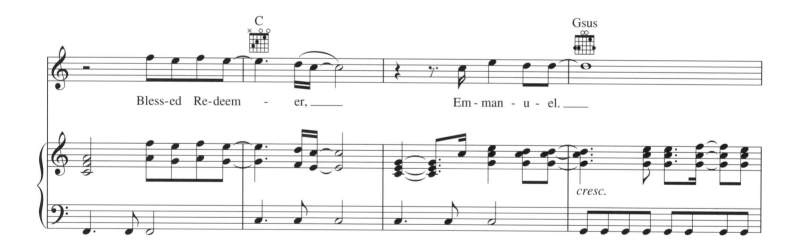

Bless-ed Re - deem - er, _____ Em - man - u - el. ____

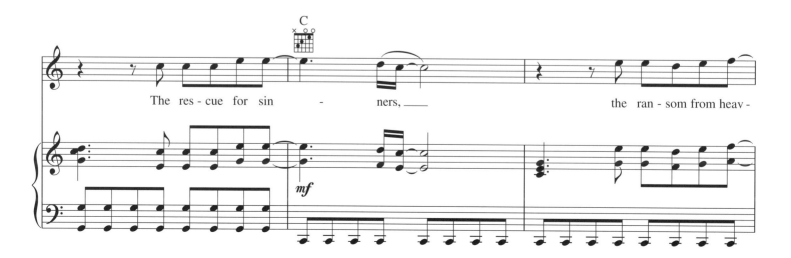

The res - cue for sin - ners, ____ the ran - som from heav-

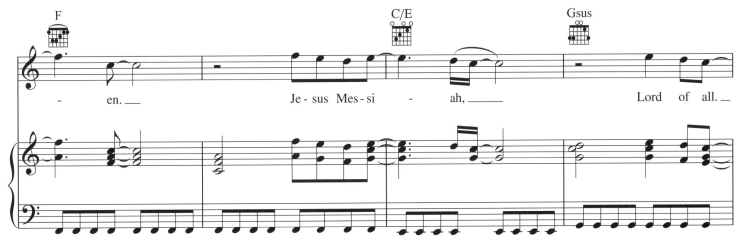

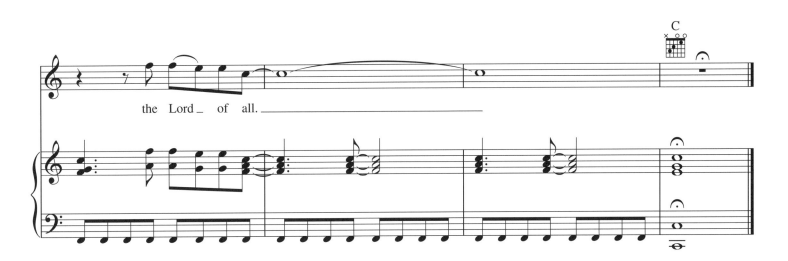

LAMB OF GOD

Words and Music by
TWILA PARIS

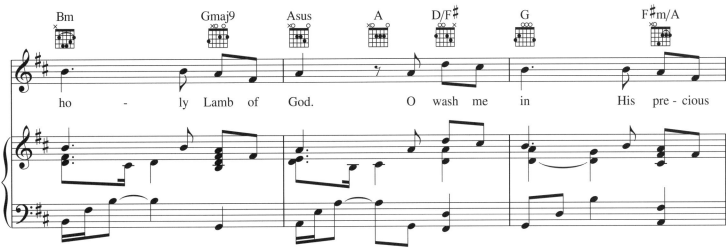

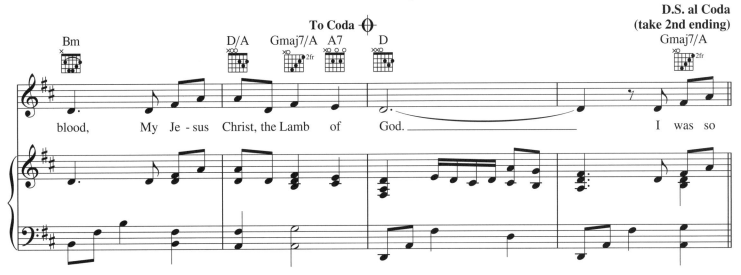

LEAD ME TO THE CROSS

Words and Music by
BROOKE FRASER

Recorded a half step lower.

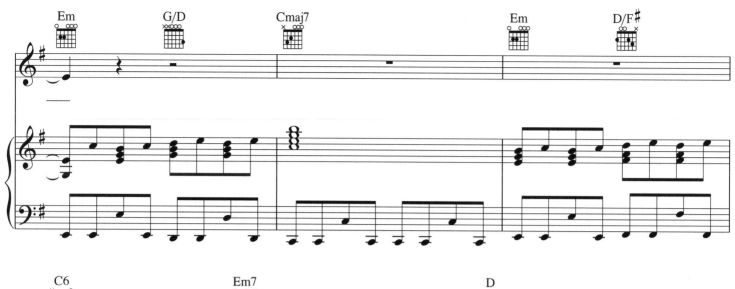

You were, as I,_____ tempt-ed and tried,__

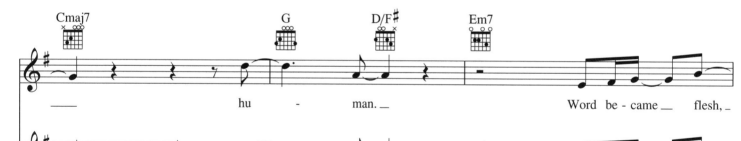

_____ hu - man. __ Word be-came __ flesh, _

_____ bore my sin and death. __ Now You're ris - en. __

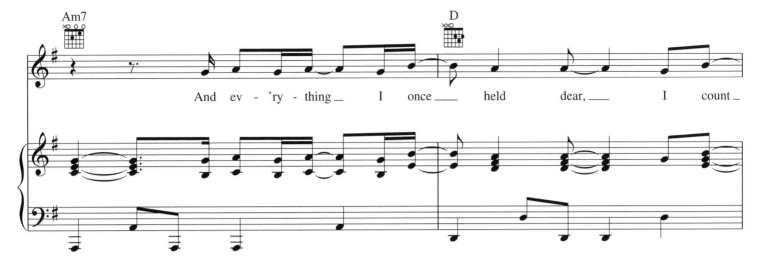

And ev - 'ry - thing ___ I once ___ held dear, ___ I count ___

D.S. al Coda

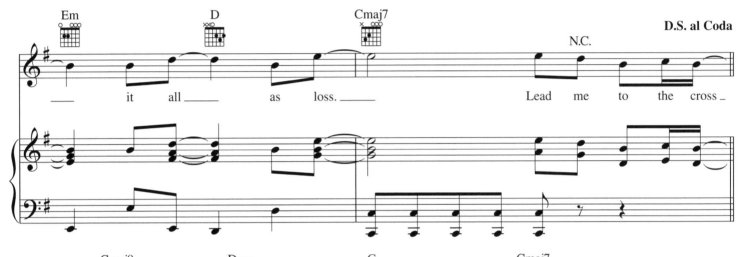

___ it all ___ as loss. ___ Lead me to the cross ___

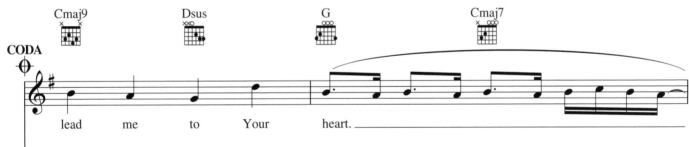

CODA

lead me to Your heart. ___

___ Lead me to ___ Your heart. ___

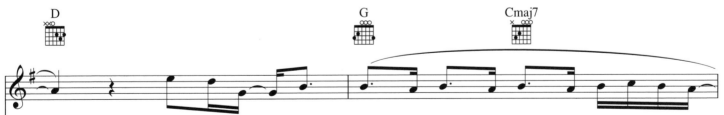

Rid me of ___ my - self. ___ I be - long to ___ You. ___

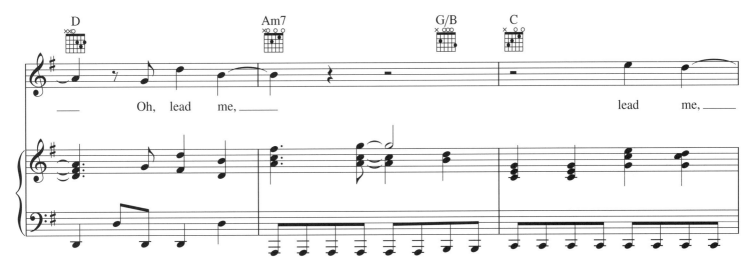

___ Oh, lead me, ___ lead me, ___

___ lead me to the cross. ___

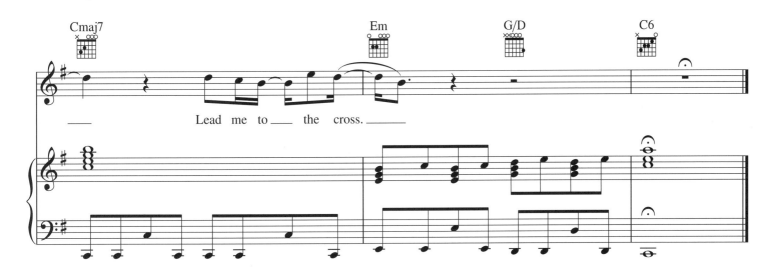

___ Lead me to ___ the cross. ___

LOST IN WONDER

Words and Music by
MARTYN LAYZELL

chose the cross __ with ev-'ry breath; __ the per-fect life, __ the per-fect death.
loosed the cords __ of sin-ful-ness, __ and broke the chains __ of my dis-grace.

You chose __ the cross. __
You chose __ the cross. __

crown of thorns __ You wore for us, __ and crowned us with __ e - ter - nal life.
from the grace __ vic - to - ri - ous, __ You rose a - gain __ so glo - ri - ous.

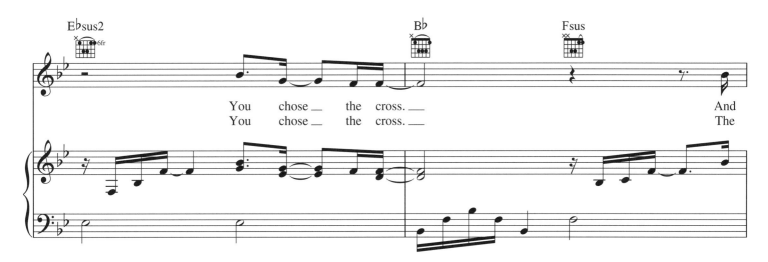

You chose __ the cross. __
You chose __ the cross. __

And
The

though Your soul __ was o - ver - whelmed __ with pain, __ o -
sor - row that __ sur - round - ed You __ was mine, __ yet,

be - di - ent __ to death, __ You o - ver - came.)
"Not My will, __ but Yours __ be done," __ You __ cried.)

I'm lost in

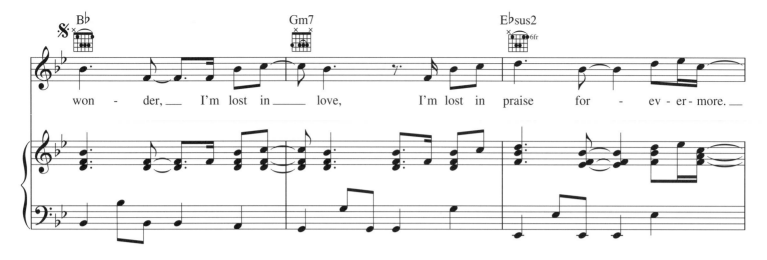

won - der, ___ I'm lost in ___ love, I'm lost in praise for - ev - er - more. ___

___ Be - cause of Je - sus' ___ un - fail - ing ___ love, I am for -

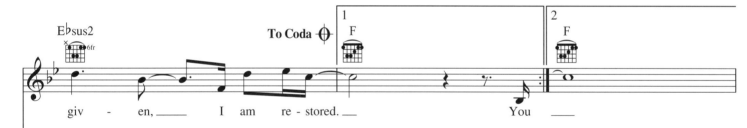

To Coda

giv - en, ___ I am re - stored. ___ You ___

And though Your soul ___ was o - ver - whelmed ___ with pain, ___ o-

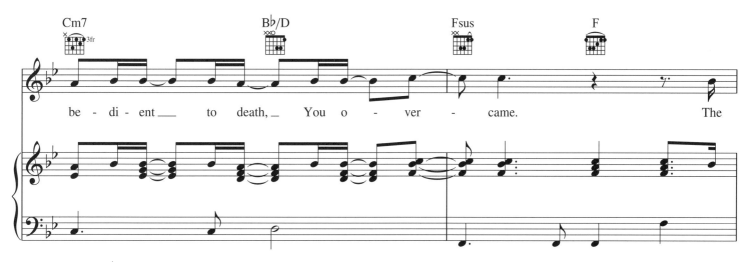

be - di - ent ___ to death, ___ You o - ver - came. The

sor - row that ___ sur - round - ed You ___ was mine, ___ yet,

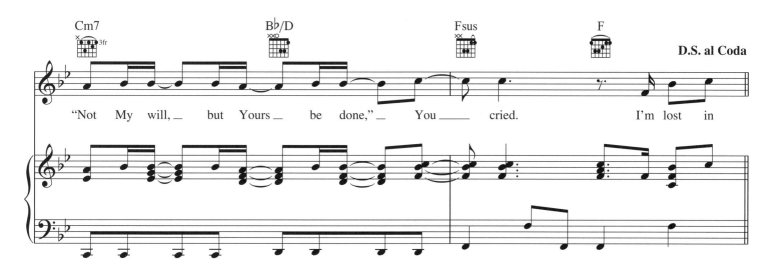

D.S. al Coda

"Not My will, ___ but Yours ___ be done," ___ You ___ cried. I'm lost in

CODA

Be - cause of Je - sus, ___ be - cause of Je - sus, ___ be - cause of

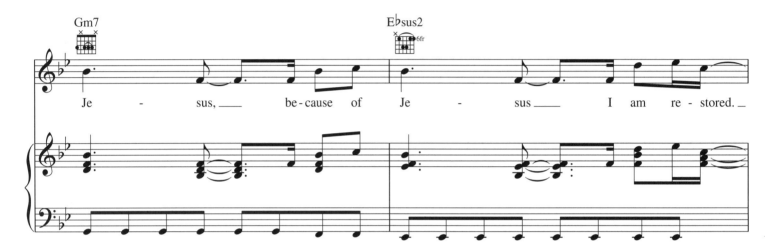

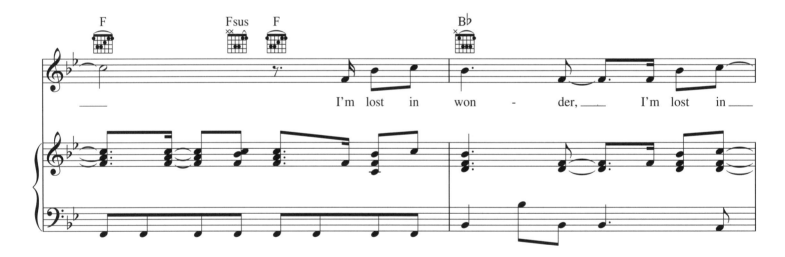

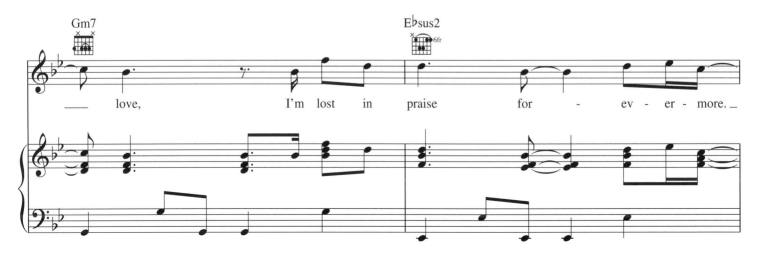

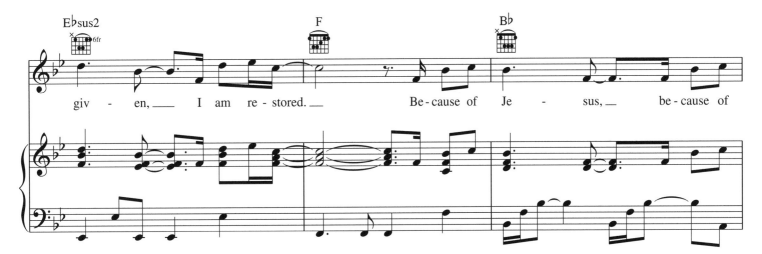

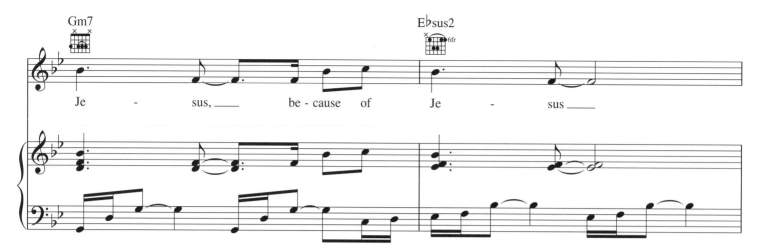

Je - sus, ____ be - cause of Je - sus ___

I'm re - stored. ___

(Vocal ad lib.)

And I'm for - giv - en. _____

Repeat ad lib.   **Final Ending**

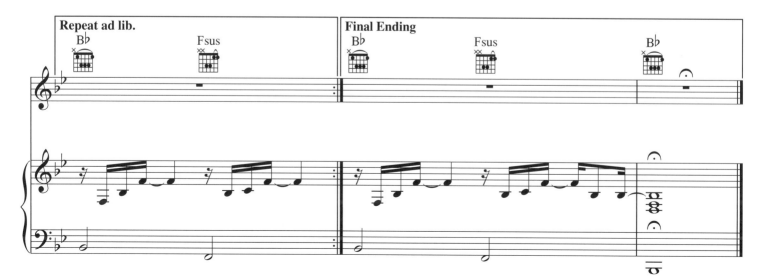

MESSAGE OF THE CROSS

Words and Music by
MARTIN SMITH

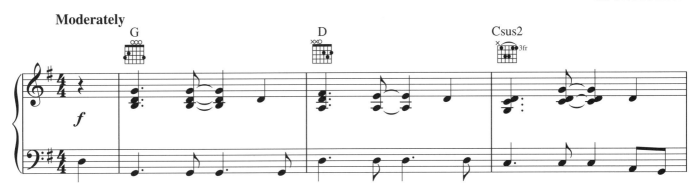

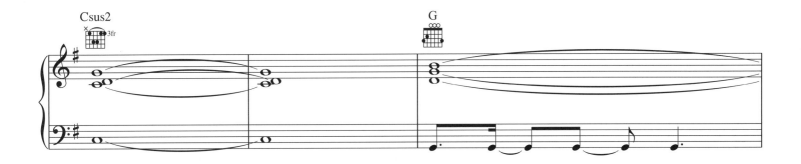

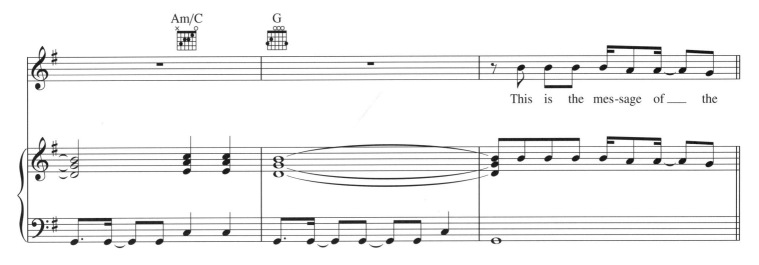

This is the mes-sage of ___ the

vealed Your __ love __ and You laid down __ Your life.
con - quered __ sin __ and You gave us __ new life.
be - ing __ saved, __ it is the pow - er __ of God.

This is the mes-sage of __ the
You set me free __ when I came to the cross, __
You set us free __ when we come to the cross. __

__ poured out Your blood __ for I was bro - ken and lost. There I was healed __
You pour out Your blood, __ for we are bro - ken and lost. Here we are healed __

__ and You cov - ered my sin. __ It's there You saved __ me, __ hey.
__ and You cov - er our sin. __ It's here You save __ us, __ yeah.

To Coda

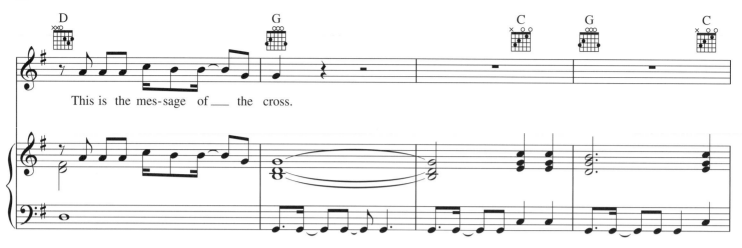

This is the mes-sage of __ the cross.

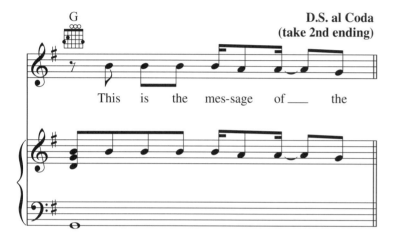

D.S. al Coda
(take 2nd ending)

This is the mes-sage of __ the

CODA

You set me free __

__ when I come to the cross, pour out Your blood __ for I am bro-ken and

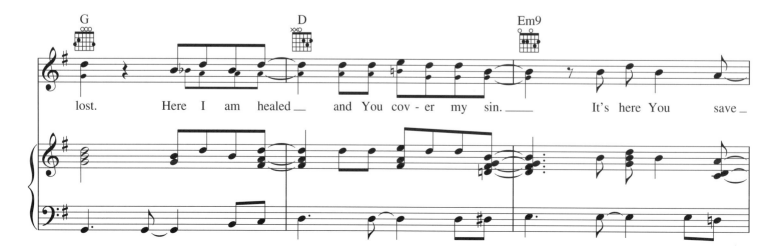

lost. Here I am healed __ and You cov-er my sin.__ It's here You save __

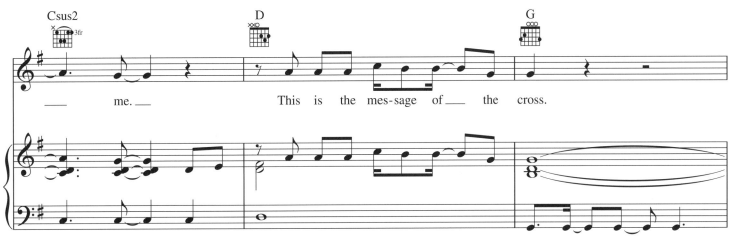

me. This is the mes-sage of ___ the cross.

Oh, yeah. Come to ___ the

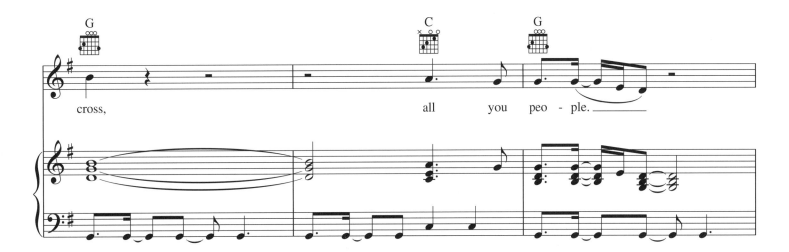

cross, all you peo - ple. _____

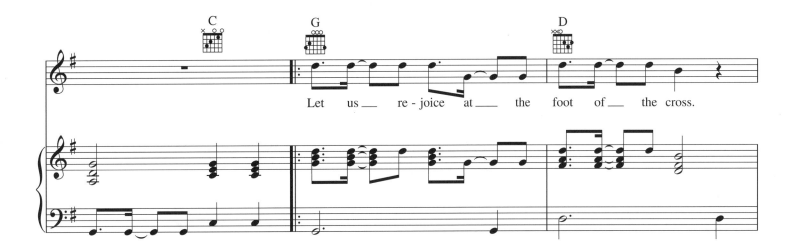

Let us ___ re - joice at ___ the foot of ___ the cross.

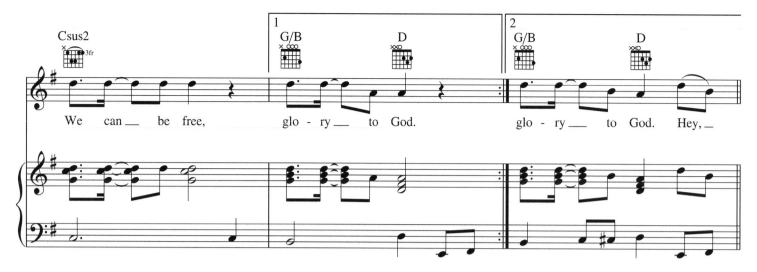

We can __ be free, glo-ry __ to God. glo-ry __ to God. Hey, __

let } us __ re-joice at __ the foot of __ the cross. We can __ be free,
Let }

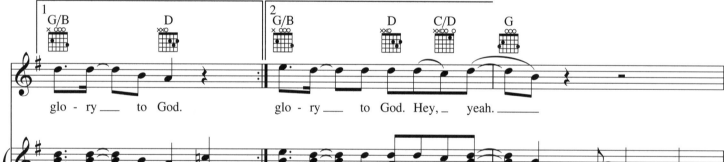

glo-ry __ to God. glo-ry __ to God. Hey, __ yeah. _____

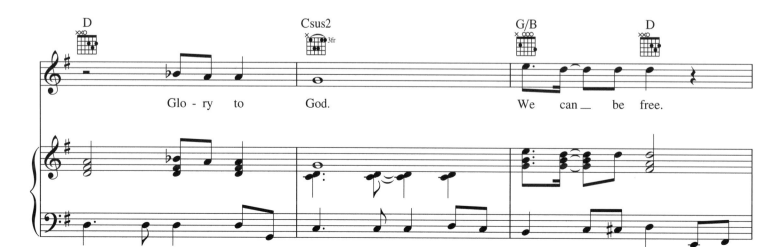

Glo-ry to God. We can __ be free.

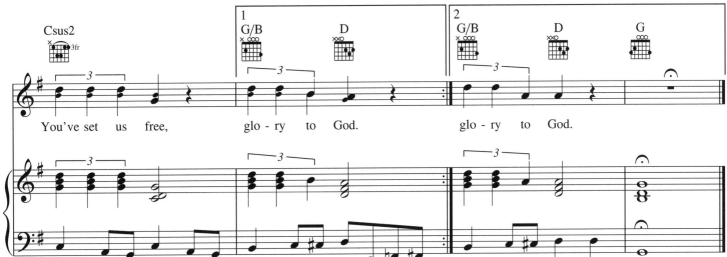

MIGHTY IS THE POWER OF THE CROSS

Words and Music by SHAWN CRAIG
and CHRIS TOMLIN

Gentle rhythm

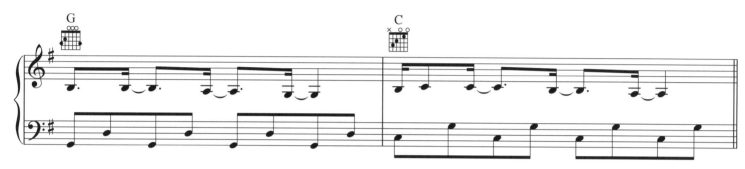

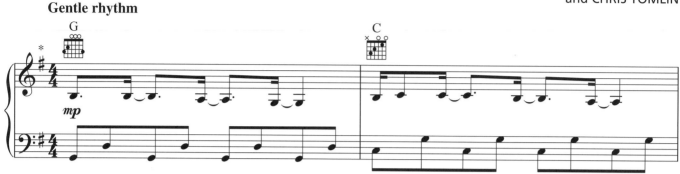

What can take ___ a dy - ing man ___ and raise him up ___ to life ___ a - gain? ___
What re - stores ___ our faith ___ in God? ___ What re - veals ___ the Fa - ther's love? ___

What can heal ___ a wound - ed soul? ___ What can make ___ us white ___ as snow? ___
What can lead ___ the way - ward home? ___ What can melt ___ a heart ___ of stone? ___

* Recorded a half step lower.

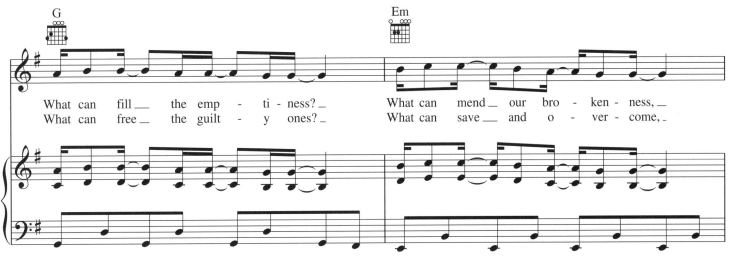

What can fill___ the emp - ti - ness?___
What can free__ the guilt - y ones?___

What can mend__ our bro - ken - ness,___
What can save__ and o - ver - come,___

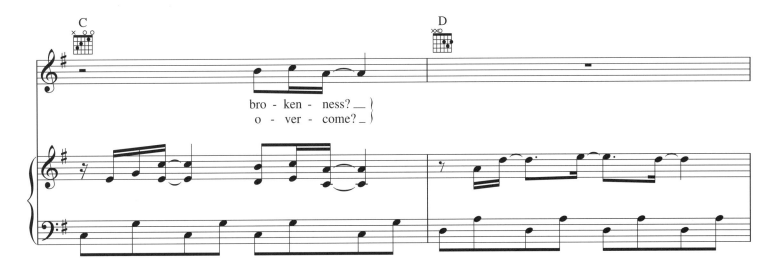

bro - ken - ness?___
o - ver - come?___

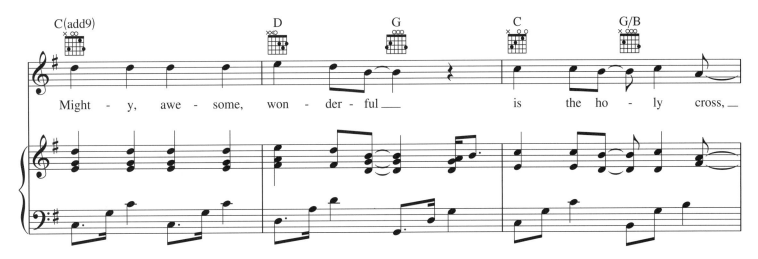

Might - y, awe - some, won - der - ful___ is the ho - ly cross,___

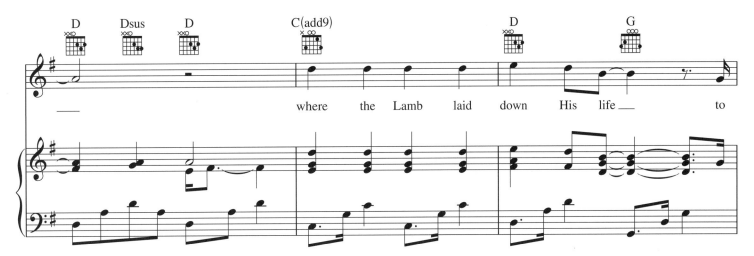

where the Lamb laid down His life___ to

lift us from ___ the fall. ___ Might - y ___ is the

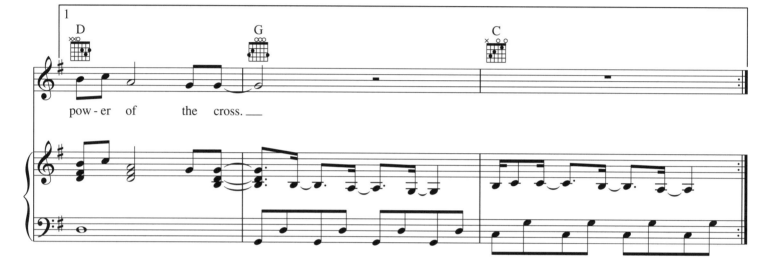

pow - er of the cross. ___

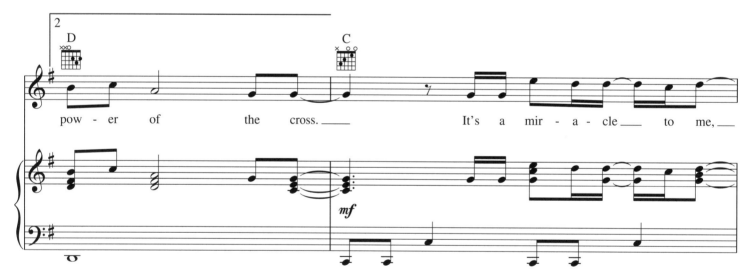

pow - er of the cross. ___ It's a mir - a - cle ___ to me, ___

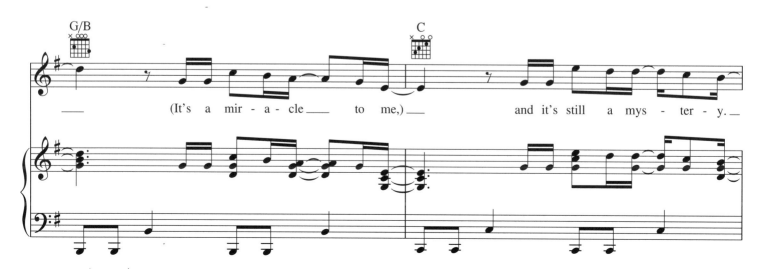

___ (It's a mir - a - cle ___ to me,) ___ and it's still a mys - ter - y. ___

(and it's still a mys - ter - y.) It's a mir - a - cle__ to me,__

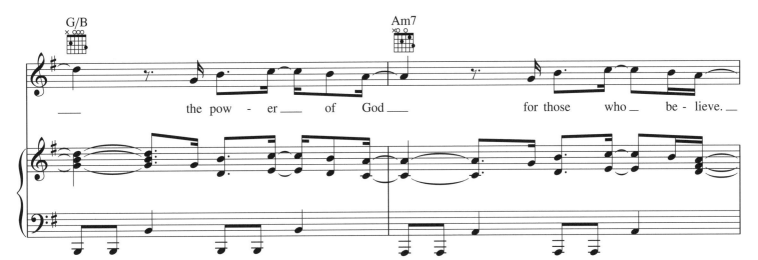

__ the pow - er__ of God__ for those who__ be - lieve.__

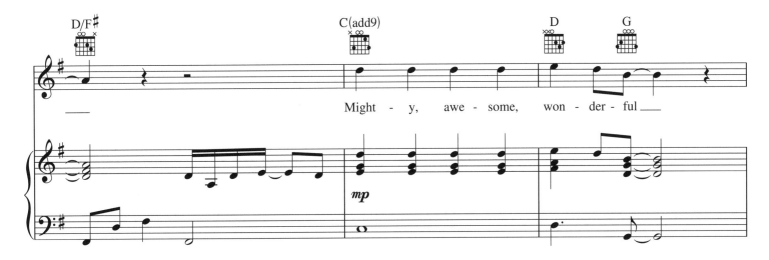

__ Might - y, awe - some, won - der - ful __

mp

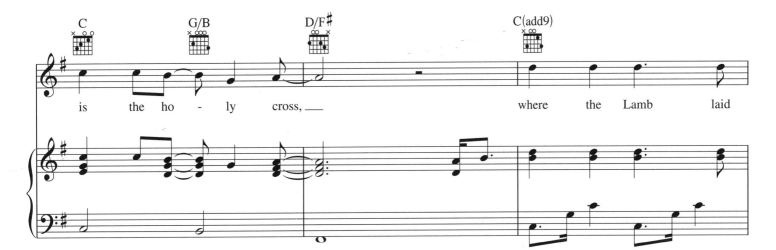

is the ho - ly cross, __ where the Lamb laid

down His life ___ to lift us from __ the fall. ___ Oh, __ and

might - y, awe - some, won - der - ful ___ is the ho - ly cross, __

__ where the Lamb laid down His life __ to

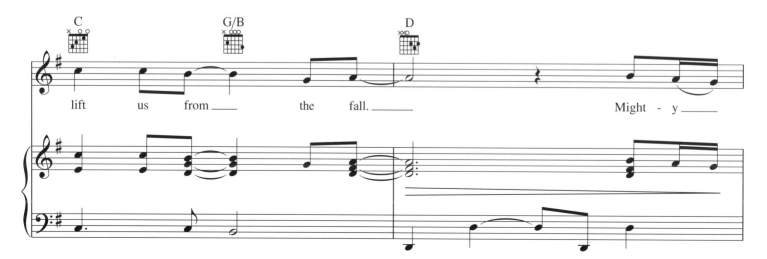

lift us from ___ the fall. ____ Might - y ____

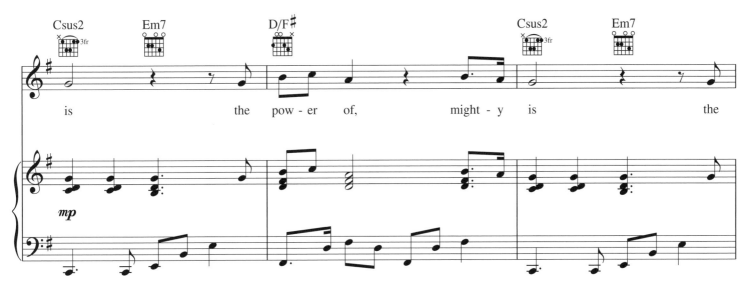

is the pow - er of, might - y is the

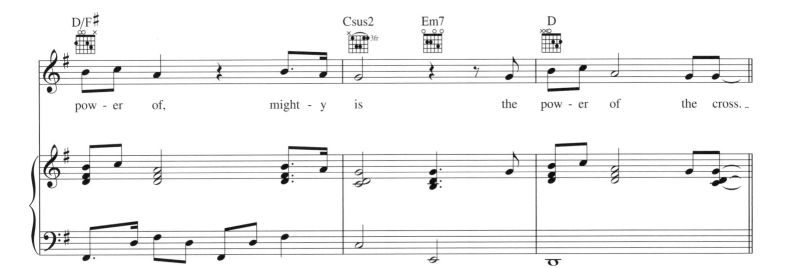

pow - er of, might - y is the pow - er of the cross. _

_____ Thank You for ___ the cross. _

Thank You for _____

_____ the cross.   I love the cross. _____

I love _ the cross. _____

NOTHING BUT THE BLOOD

Words and Music by
MATT REDMAN

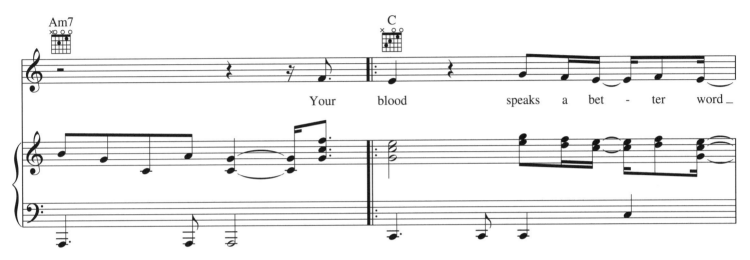

Your blood ___ speaks a bet - ter word ___

___ than all the emp - ty claims ___ I've heard up - on ___ this earth, ___

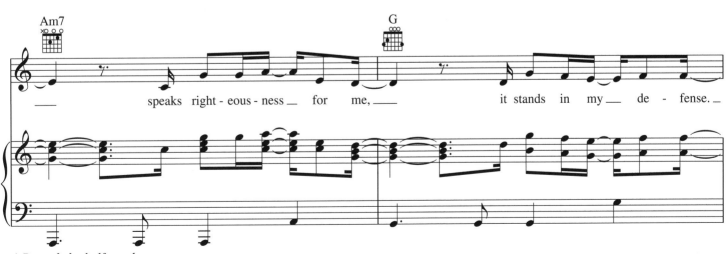

___ speaks right - eous - ness ___ for me, ___ it stands in my ___ de - fense.

Recorded a half step lower.

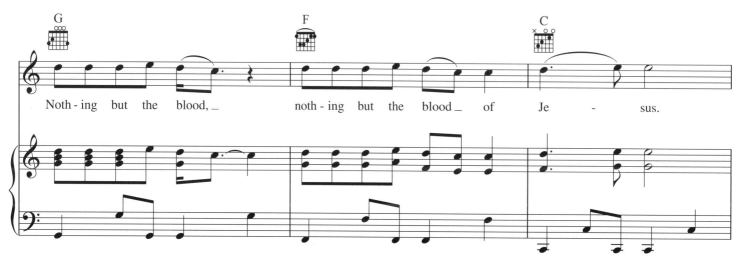

What can wash — us pure — as snow, —

wel - comed as — the friends — of God? — Noth - ing but Your blood, —

noth - ing but Your blood, — King Je - sus.

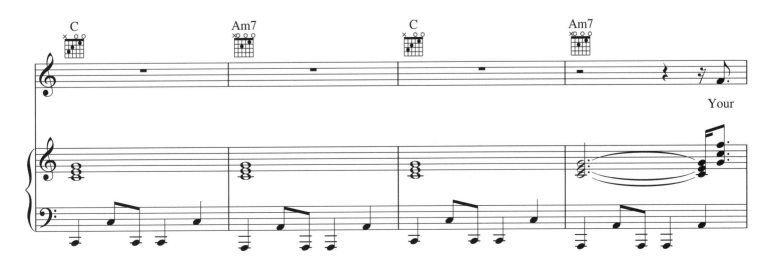

Your

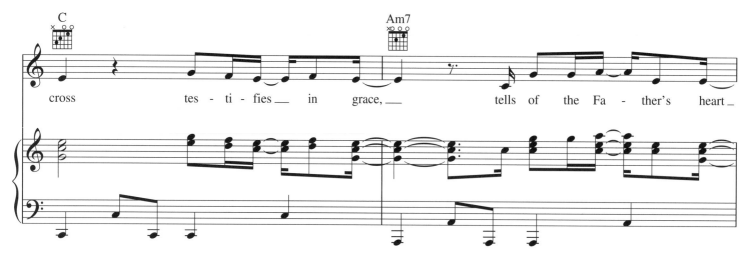

cross   tes - ti - fies __ in   grace, __   tells of the Fa - ther's heart __

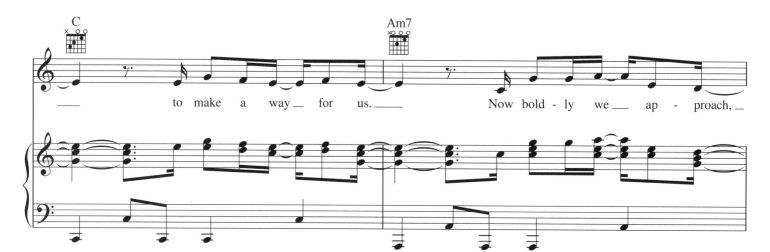

__   to make a way __ for us. __   Now bold - ly we __ ap - proach, __

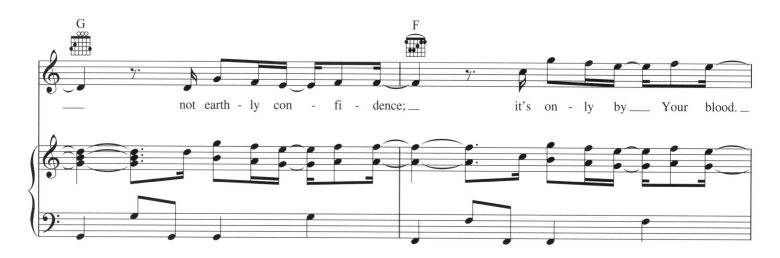

__   not earth - ly con - fi - dence; __   it's on - ly by __ Your blood. __

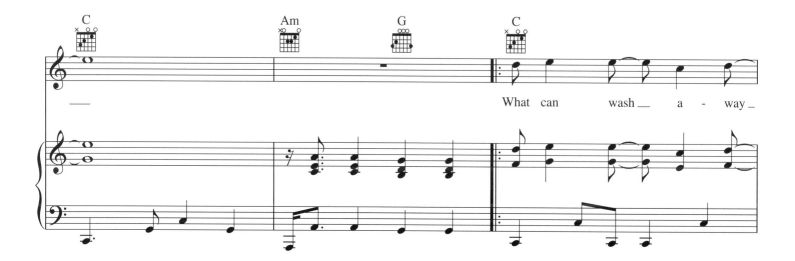

__   What can wash __ a - way __

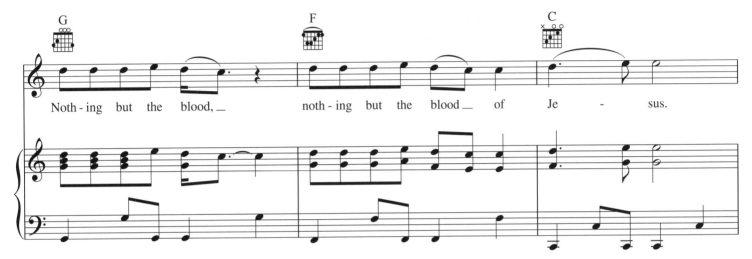

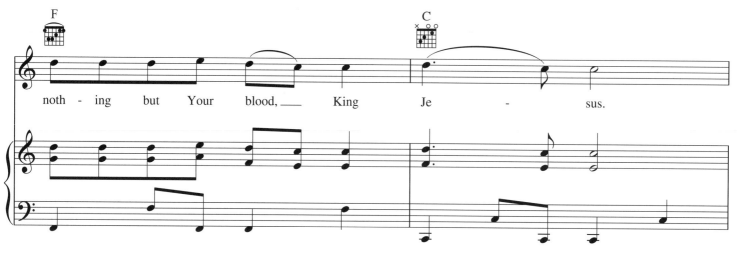

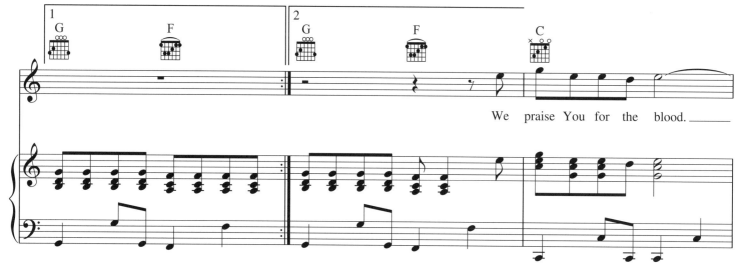

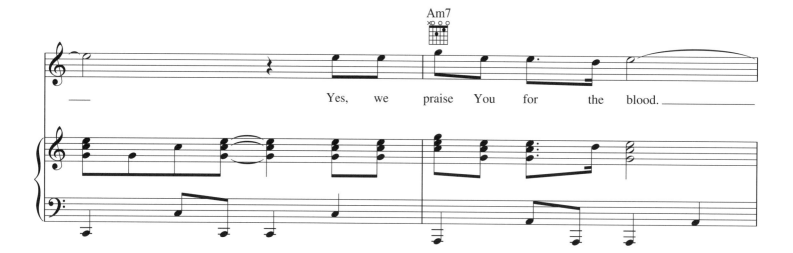

stored and for - giv - en. ___ Thank You, Lord. We

praise You for the blood. _____ We praise You for the blood.

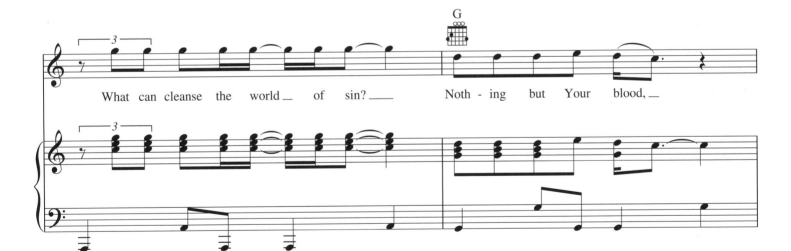

What can cleanse the world __ of sin? ___ Noth - ing but Your blood, __

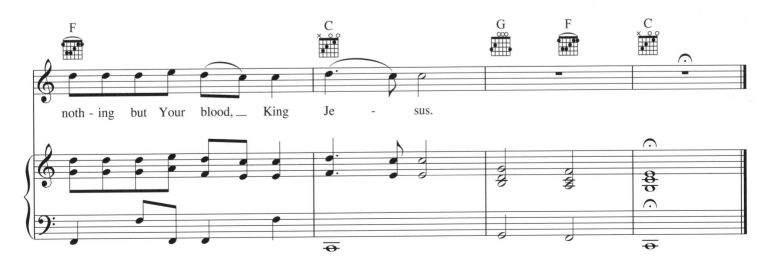

noth - ing but Your blood, __ King Je - sus.

ONCE AGAIN

Words and Music by
MATT REDMAN

Moderately

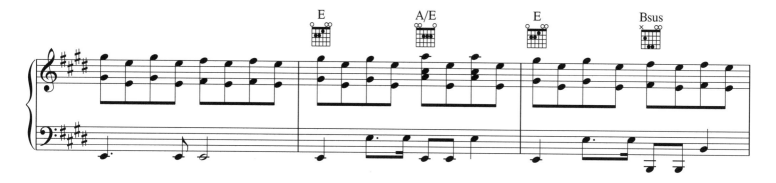

Je - sus Christ, _ I
Now You are _ ex -

think up - on Your sac - ri - fice; You be - came noth - ing, poured out to death. _
alt - ed to the high - est place, King of the heav - ens, where one day I'll bow. _

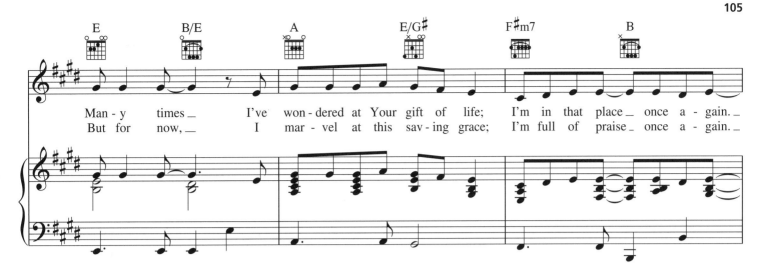

Man - y times __ I've won - dered at Your gift of life; I'm in that place __ once a - gain.
But for now, __ I mar - vel at this sav - ing grace; I'm full of praise __ once a - gain. __

__ I'm in that place __ once a - gain. __
__ I'm full of praise __ once a - gain. __

And

once a - gain I look up - on the cross where You died. __ I'm hum - bled by Your mer - cy __ and I'm

bro - ken in - side. __ Once a - gain I thank You, __ once a - gain I pour out my life. __

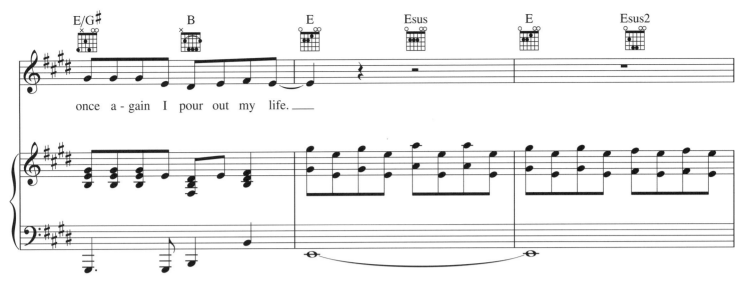

once a-gain I pour out my life. ___

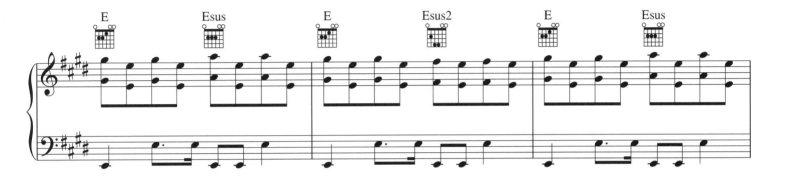

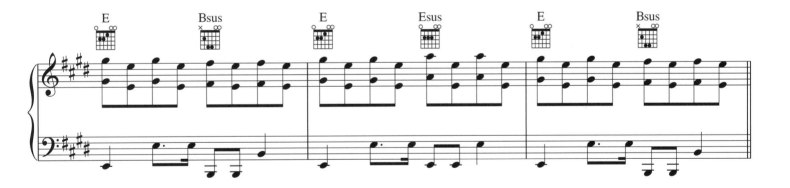

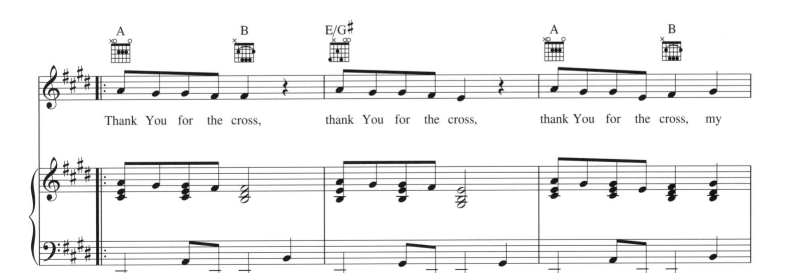

Thank You for the cross,   thank You for the cross,   thank You for the cross, my

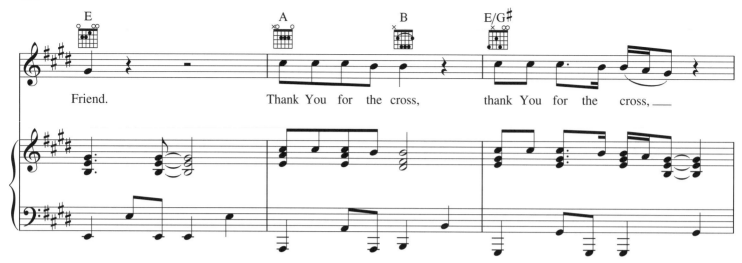

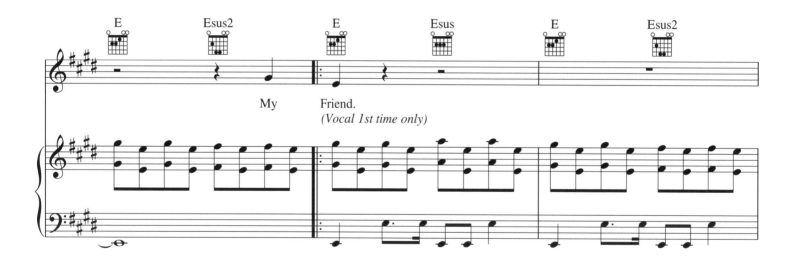

REDEEMER, SAVIOR, FRIEND

Words and Music by DARRELL EVANS
and CHRIS SPRINGER

* *Recorded a half step lower.*

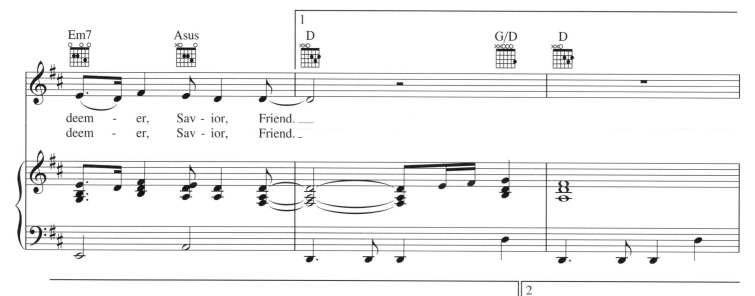

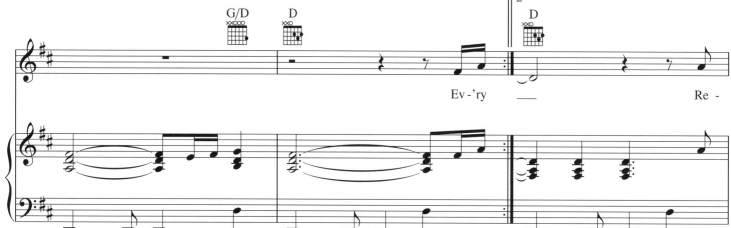

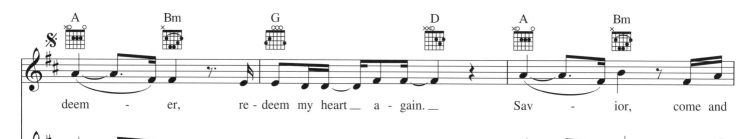

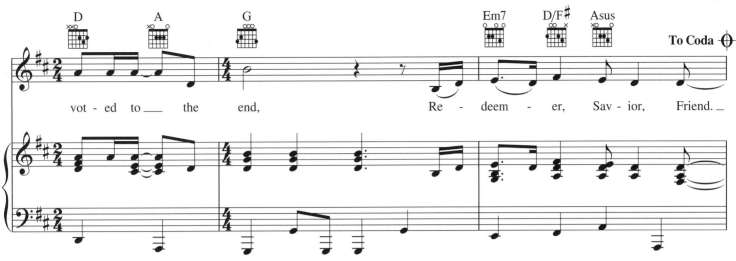

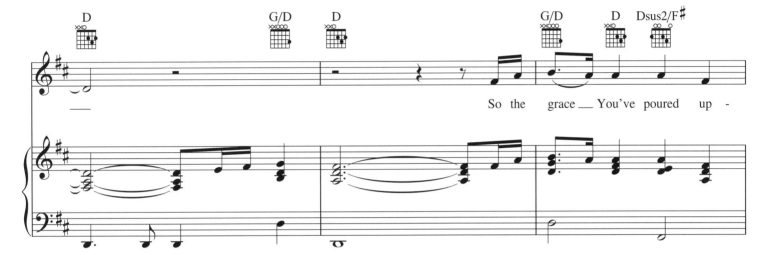

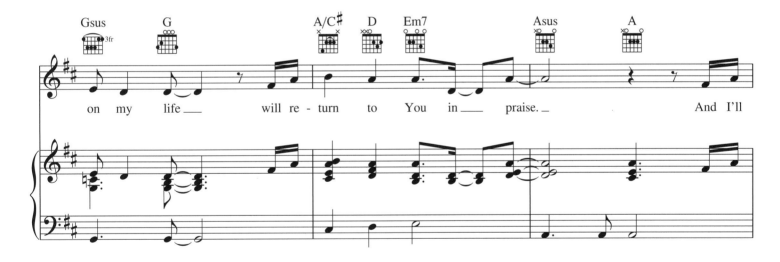

for the name ___ by which I'm saved. ___ Re -

CODA

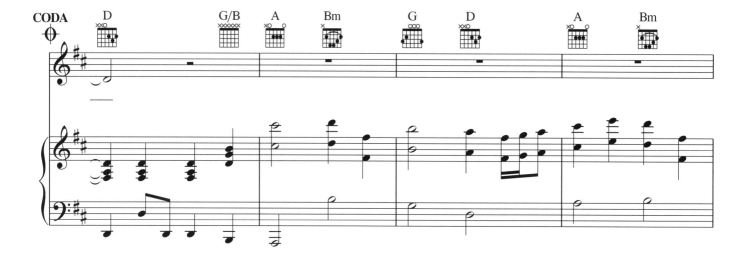

Re - deem ___ er, re - deem my heart ___ a - gain. ___

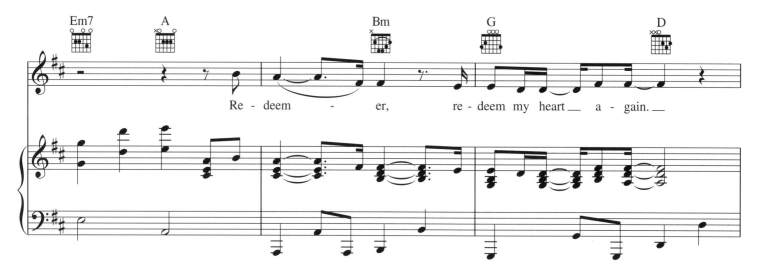

Sav - ior, come and shel - ter me ___ from sin. ___ You're fa -

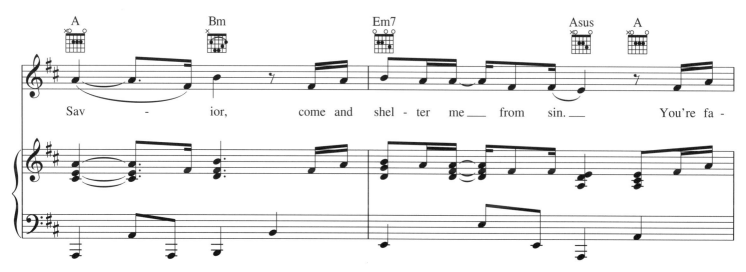

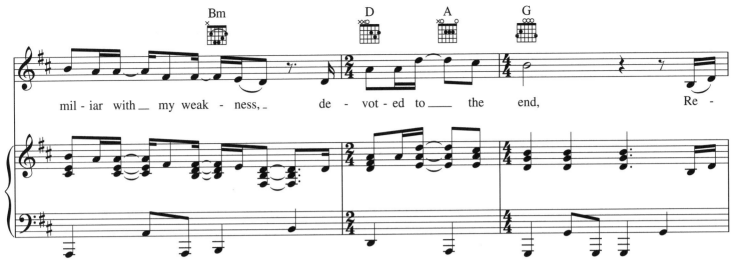

mil - iar with __ my weak - ness, __ de - vot - ed to __ the end, __ Re -

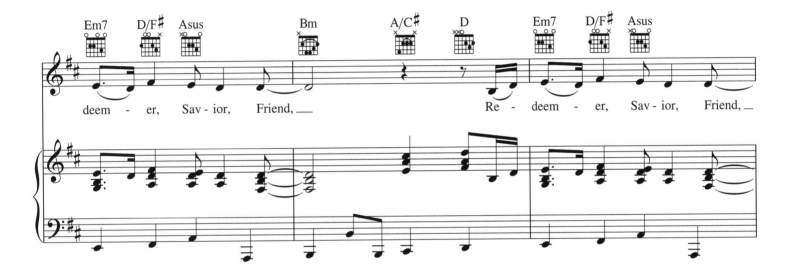

deem - er, Sav - ior, Friend, __ Re - deem - er, Sav - ior, Friend, __

__ Re - deem - er, Sav - ior, Friend. __

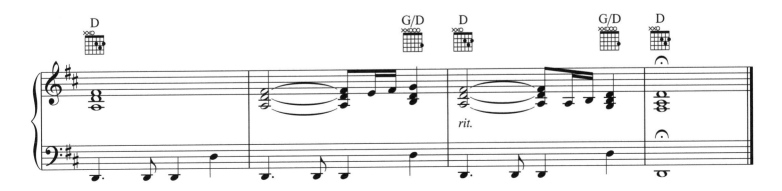

rit.

THE POWER OF THE CROSS
(Oh to See the Dawn)

Words and Music by KEITH GETTY
and STUART TOWNEND

Slowly, with freedom

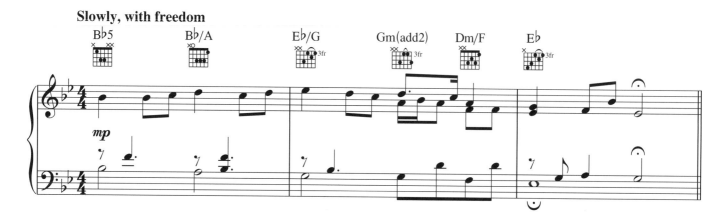

Moderately slow

Oh, to see the dawn of the dark-est day, Christ on the road to
Oh, to see the pain writ-ten on Your face, bear-ing the awe-some
Now the day-light flees, now the ground be-neath quakes as its Mak-er

Cal-va-ry. Tried by sin-ful men, torn and beat-en, then
weight of ___ sin. Ev-'ry bit-ter thought, ev-'ry e-vil deed,
bows His ___ head. Cur-tain torn in two, dead are raised to life,

at the cross.

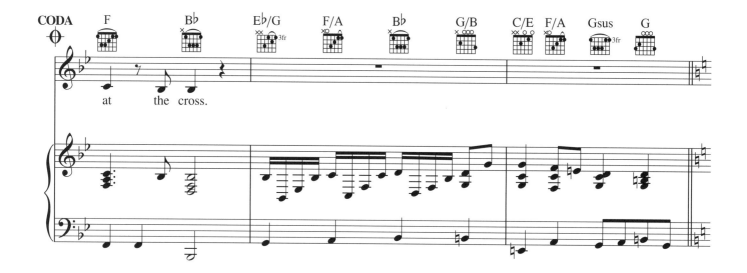

Oh, to see my name writ - ten in the wounds, for through Your suf - f'ring

I am ___ free. Death is crushed to death, life is mine to live,

won through Your self - less ___ love. This, the pow'r of the

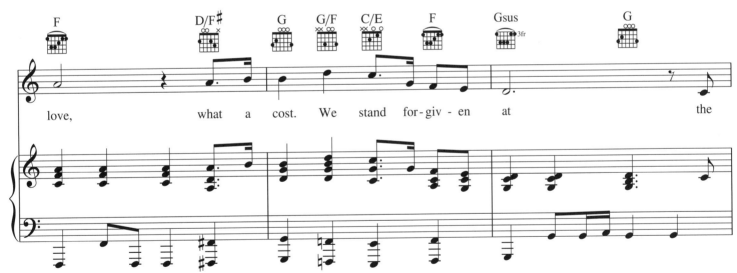

cross: Son of God slain for us. What a

love, what a cost. We stand for-giv-en at the

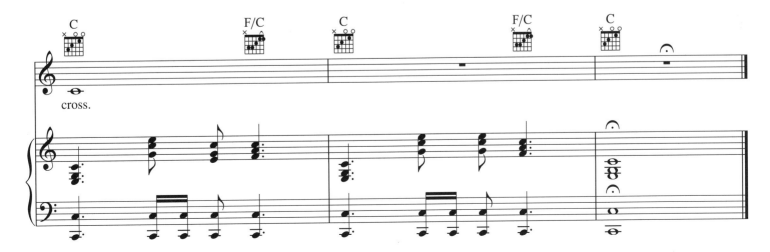

cross.

SAVIOUR KING

Words and Music by MARTY SAMPSON
and MIA FIELDES

Worshipfully

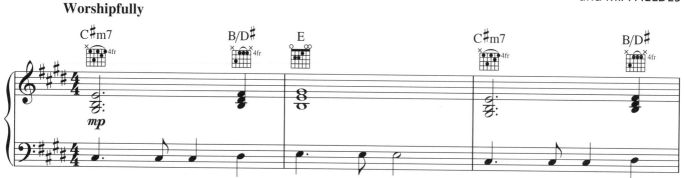

Let now the weak church say I have strength,
say shine as Your bride

by the Spir - it of pow'r that ___ raised Christ from the
that you saw in your heart as You of - fered up Your

dead. Let now the poor stand and con - fess
life. Let now the lost be wel - comed home

that my por - tion is Him

and I'm more than
by the saved and re - deemed, those a - dopt - ed as Your

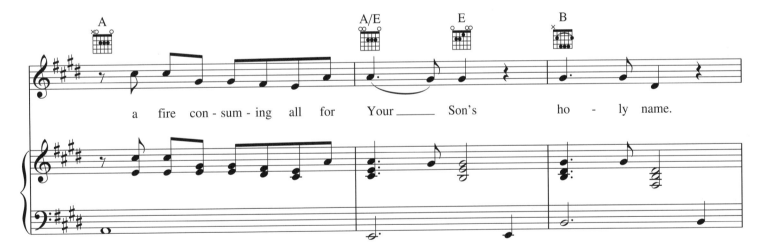

blessed.
own.

Let now our hearts burn with a flame,

a fire con - sum - ing all for Your ___ Son's ho - ly name.

And with the heav - ens we de - clare: ___ You are ___ our ___ King. ___

We love You, Lord. We wor - ship

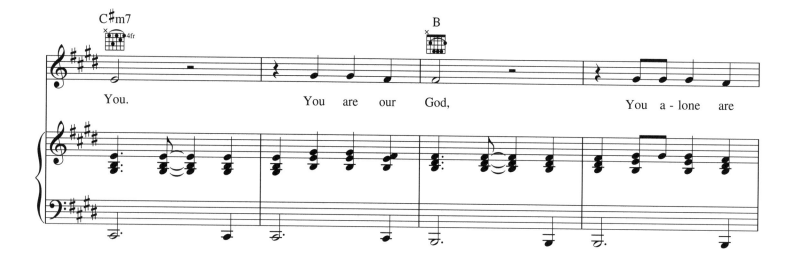

You. You are our God, You a - lone are

good. Let now Your You asked Your

Son to car - ry this:

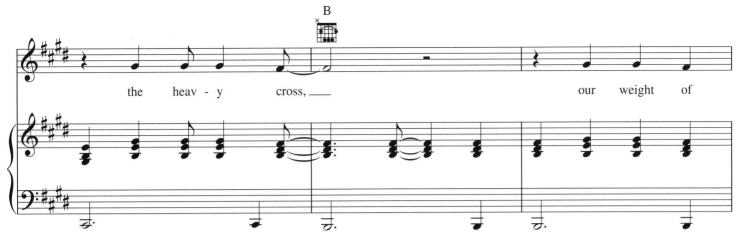

the heav-y cross, ___ our weight of

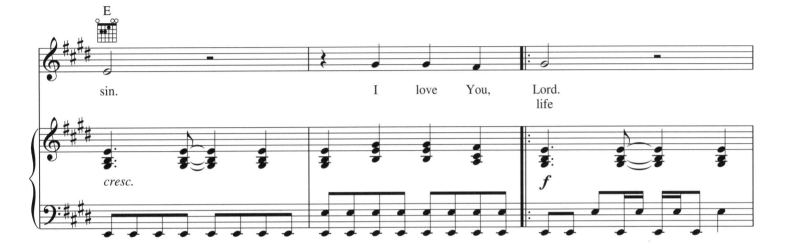

sin. I love You, Lord.
life

I wor-ship You. Hope which was lost ___
to hon-or this: the love of Christ, _

To Coda ⊕

___ now stands re-newed.
___ the Sav-iour King.

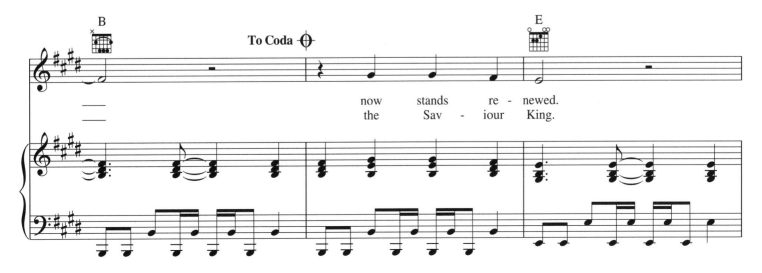

I give my

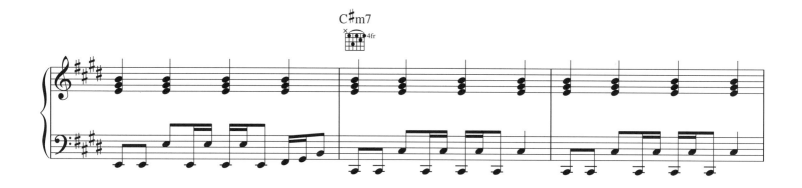

C#m7

B   Esus2

Esus   D.S. al Coda   CODA   E

the Sav - iour King.

rit.

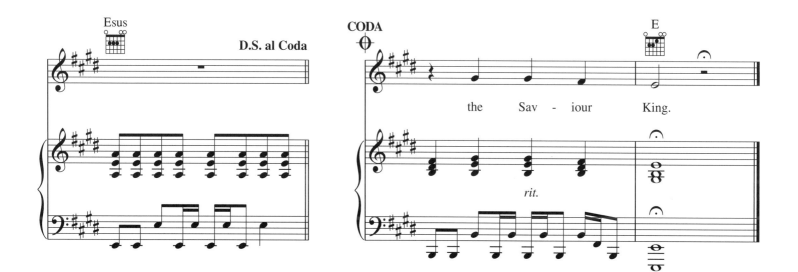

THANK YOU FOR THE BLOOD

Words and Music by
MATT REDMAN

Bright Rock

Thank you, thank you for the blood that You shed.

Stand - ing in its bless - ing, we sing these free - dom songs.

Thank you, thank you for the bat - tle You won.

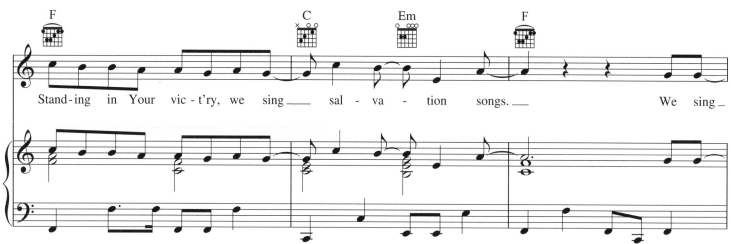

Stand-ing in Your vic-t'ry, we sing____ sal - va - tion songs.____ We sing____

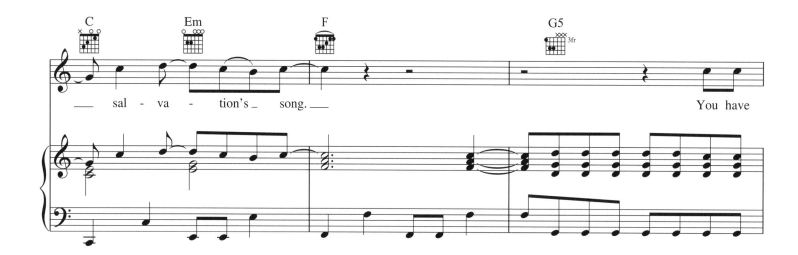

____ sal - va - tion's ___ song. ____ You have

o - pened a way to the Fa - ther where be - fore we could nev - er ___ have

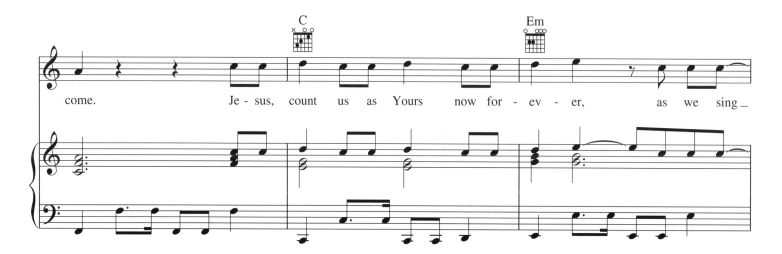

come. Je - sus, count us as Yours now for - ev - er, as we sing____

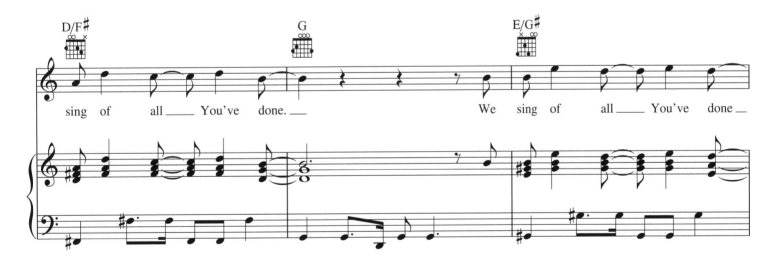

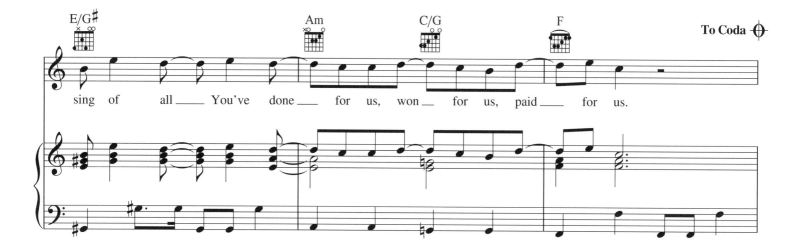

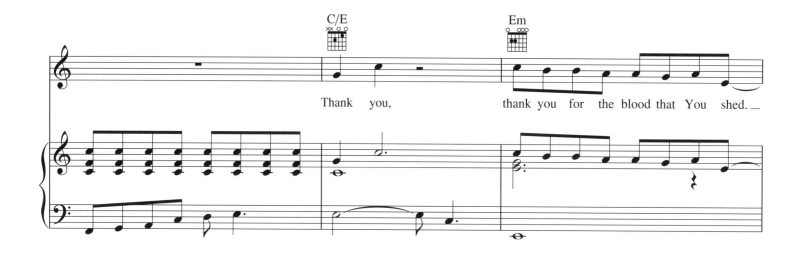

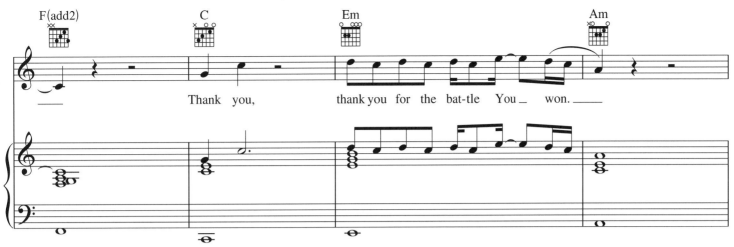

Thank you, thank you for the bat-tle You won.

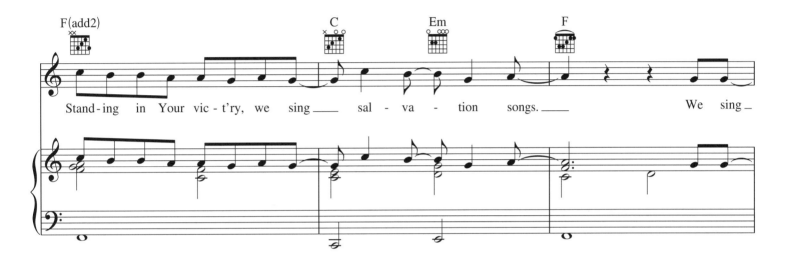

Stand-ing in Your vic-t'ry, we sing sal-va-tion songs. We sing

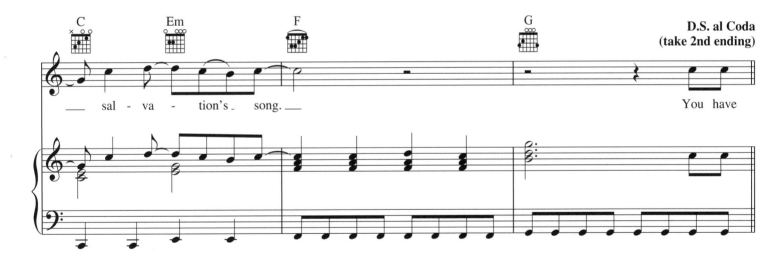

D.S. al Coda
(take 2nd ending)

sal-va-tion's song. You have

CODA

We sing of all that You've done

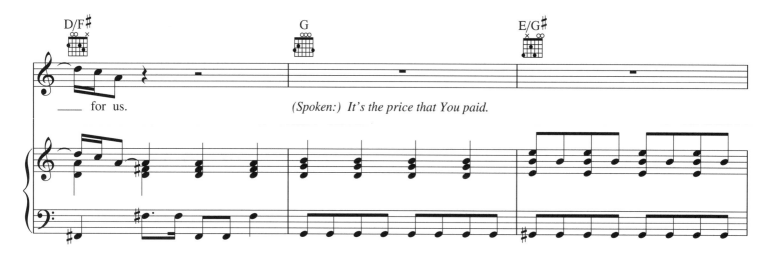

_____ for us.

(Spoken:) It's the price that You paid.

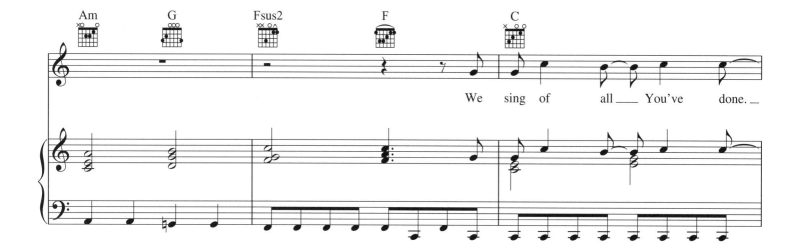

We sing of all ____ You've done. ____

____ Oh, we sing of all ____ You've done. ____ We

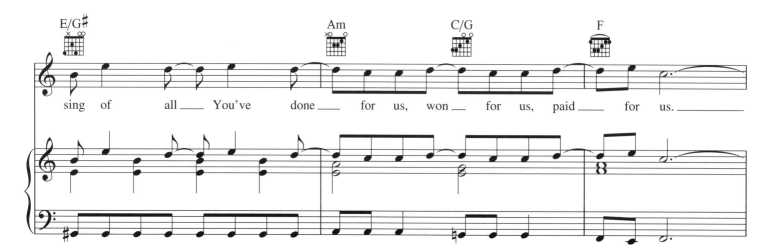

sing of all ____ You've done ____ for us, won ____ for us, paid ____ for us. ____

Yes, Lord. _____ Yes, Lord. __

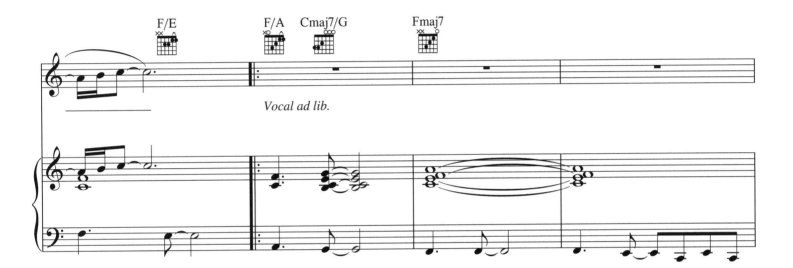

F/E   F/A   Cmaj7/G   Fmaj7

Vocal ad lib.

Play 5 times   Fsus2

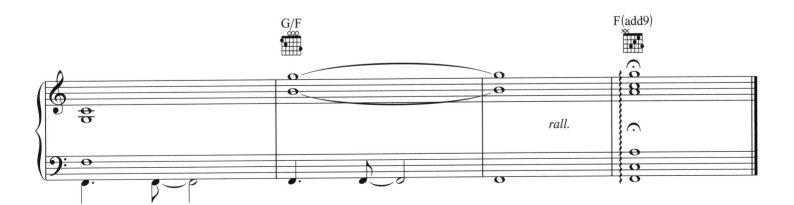

G/F   F(add9)

rall.

THE SERVANT KING
(From Heaven You Came)

Words and Music by
GRAHAM KENDRICK

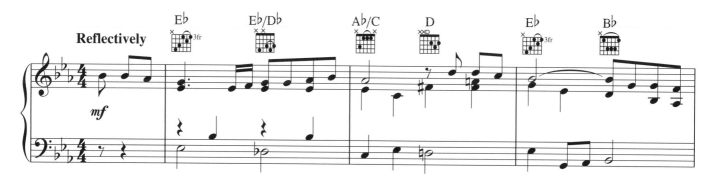

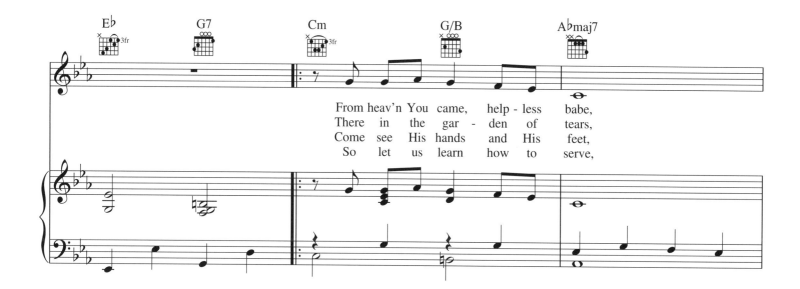

From heav'n You came, help - less babe,
There in the gar - den of tears,
Come see His hands and His feet,
So let us learn how to serve,

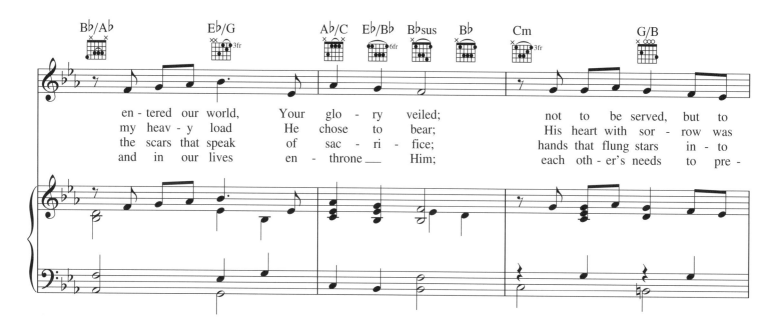

en - tered our world, Your glo - ry veiled; not to be served, but to
my heav - y load He chose to bear; His heart with sor - row was
the scars that speak of sac - ri - fice; hands that flung stars in - to
and in our lives en - throne ___ Him; each oth - er's needs to pre -

THE STAND

Words and Music by
JOEL HOUSTON

With conviction

You stood be - fore ___ cre - a - tion, e -

ter - ni - ty in ___ Your ___ hands. ___ And You spoke the earth ___ in - to mo -

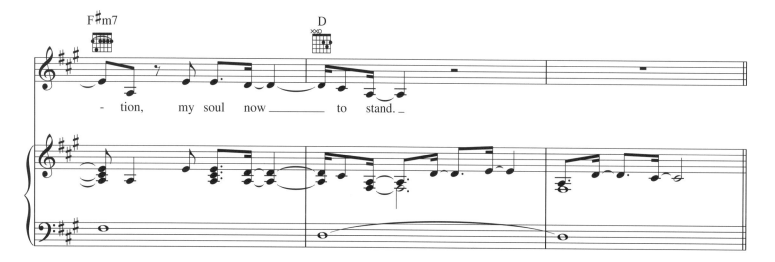

- tion, my soul now ___ to stand. ___

You stood be - fore _____ my fail - ure,
I walk up - on _____ sal - va - tion,
and Your

car - ried the cross _____ for my shame. _____
Spir - it a - live _____ in me. _____
My
This

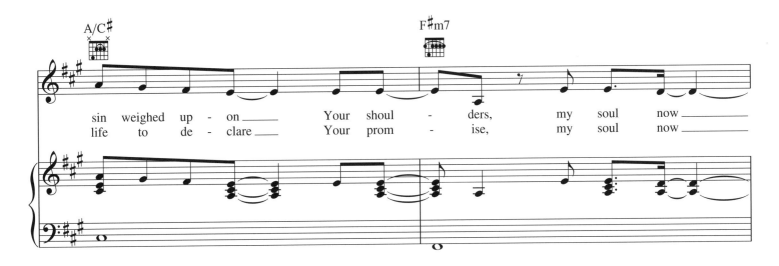

sin weighed up - on _____ Your shoul - ders, my soul now _____
life to de - clare _____ Your prom - ise, my soul now _____

_____ to stand. _____
_____ to stand. _____
So what could I _____ say? _____

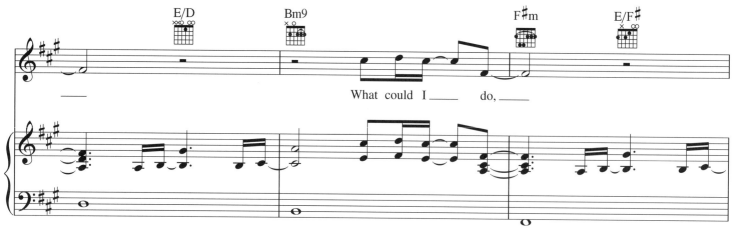

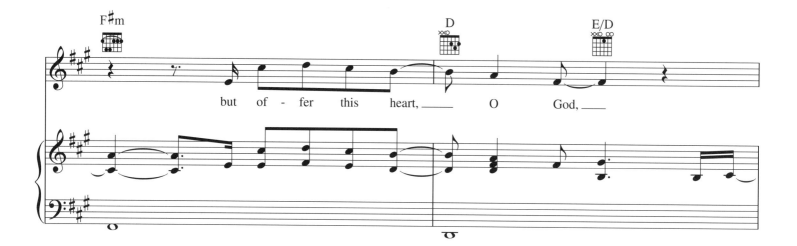

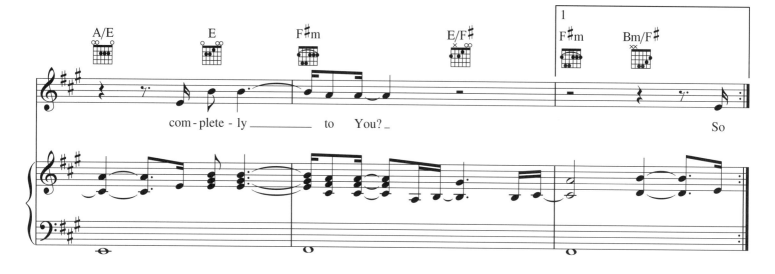

And what could I ____ do, ____ but of - fer this heart, _

____ O God, ____ com - plete - ly _____ to You? _

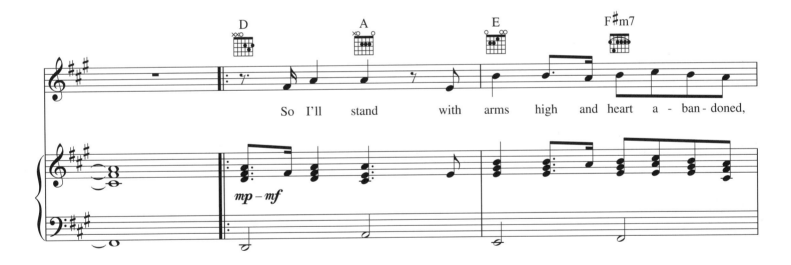

So I'll stand with arms high and heart a - ban - doned,

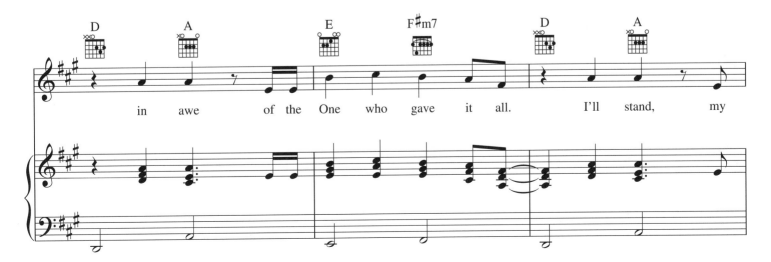

in awe of the One who gave it all. I'll stand, my

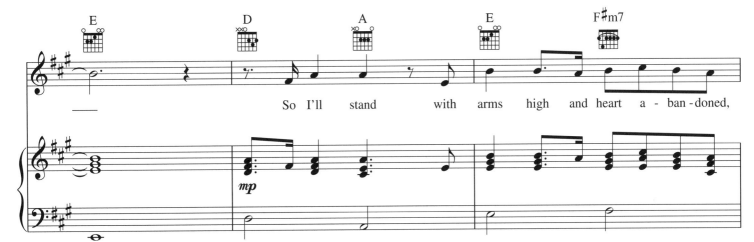

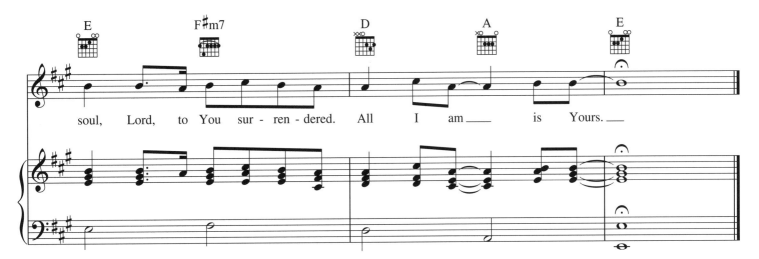

THE WONDER OF THE CROSS

Words and Music by
VICKY BEECHING

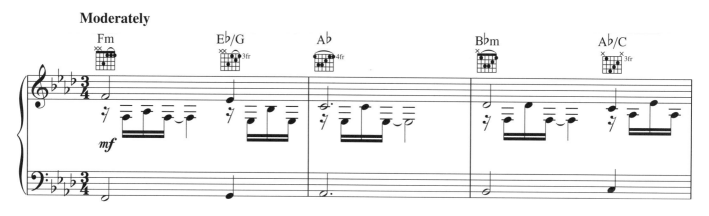

Moderately

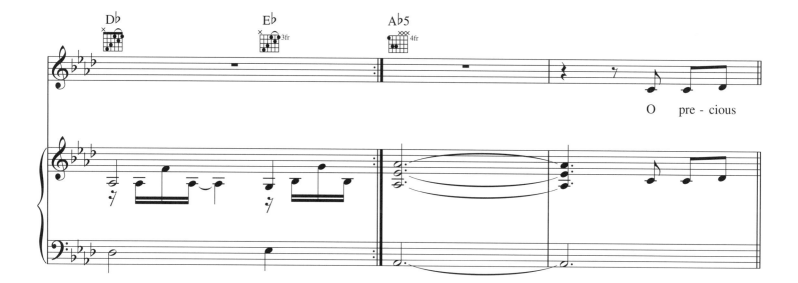

O pre - cious

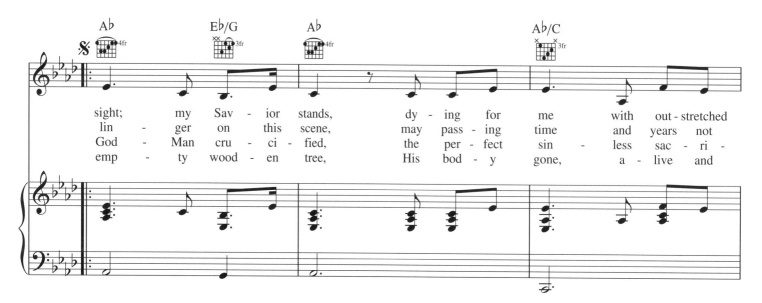

sight; my Sav - ior stands, dy - ing for me with out - stretched
lin - ger on this scene, may pass - ing time and years not
God - Man cru - ci - fied, the per - fect sin - less sac - ri -
emp - ty wood - en tree, His bod - y gone, a - live and

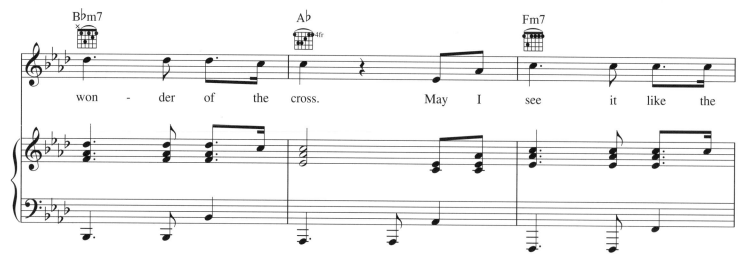

won - der of the cross. May I see it like the

first ___ time, stand - ing as a sin - ner lost, un - done by

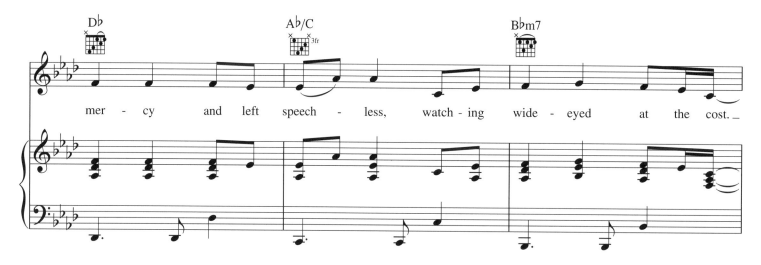

mer - cy and left speech - less, watch - ing wide - eyed at the cost. ___

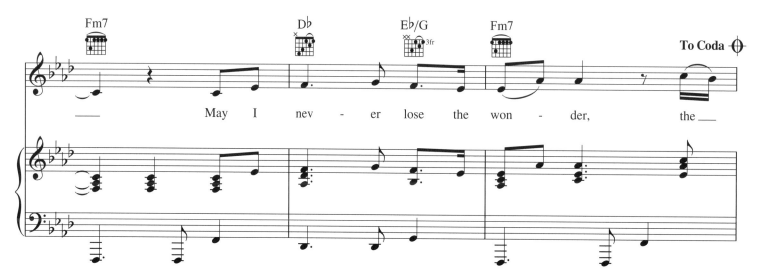

___ May I nev - er lose the won - der, the ___

D.S. al Coda

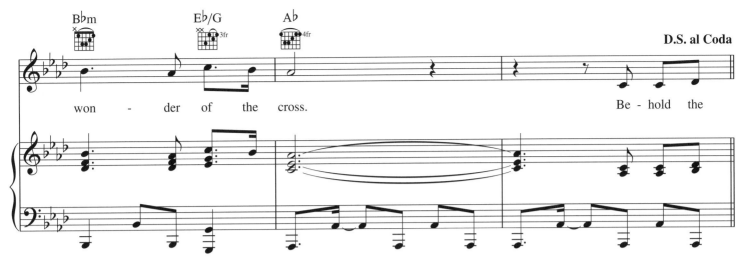

won - der of the cross. Be - hold the

CODA

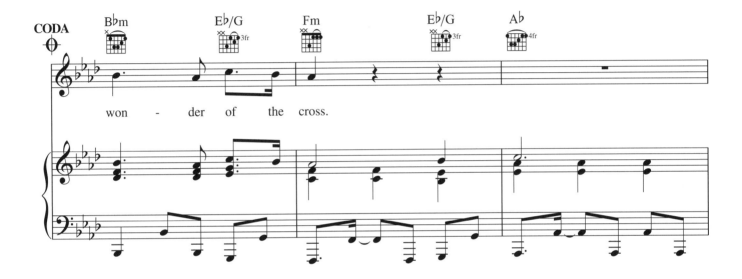

won - der of the cross.

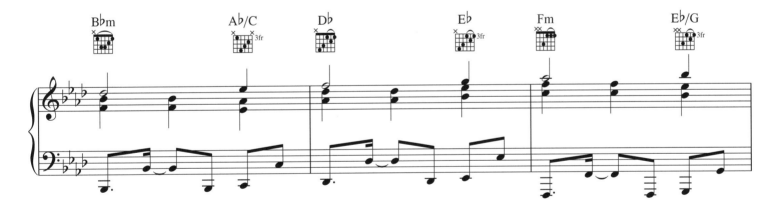

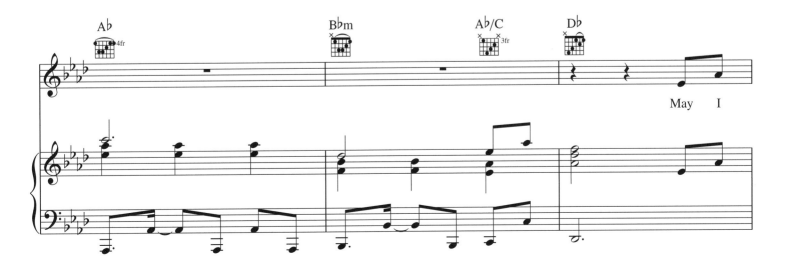

May I

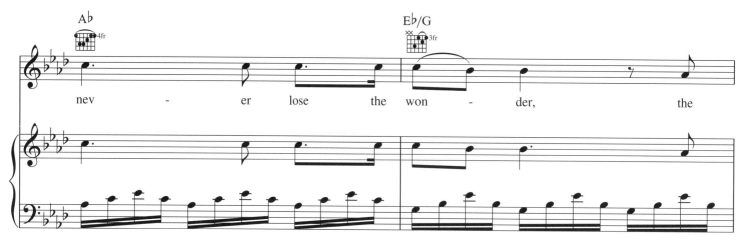

nev - er lose the won - der, the

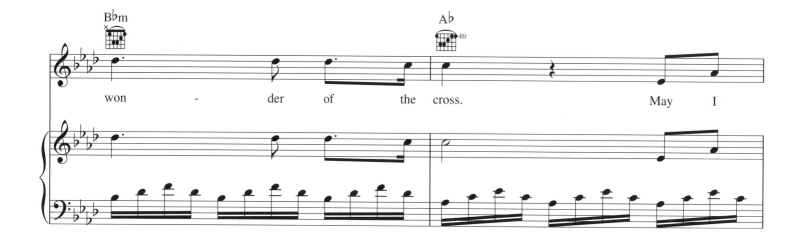

won - der of the cross. May I

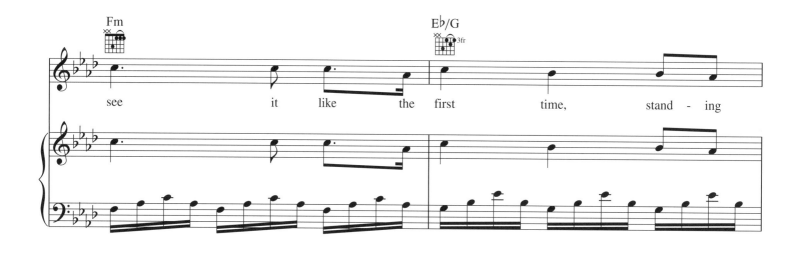

see it like the first time, stand - ing

as a sin - ner lost, un - done by

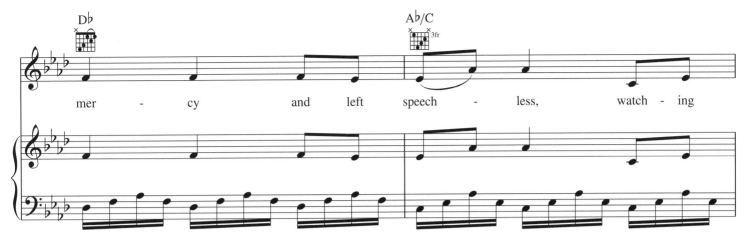

mer - cy and left speech - less, watch - ing

wide - eyed at the cost, ___ and may I

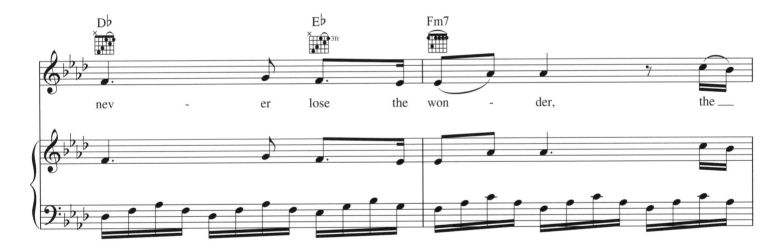

nev - er lose the won - der, the ___

won - der of the cross.

THE WONDERFUL CROSS

Words and Music by JESSE REEVES,
CHRIS TOMLIN and J.D. WALT

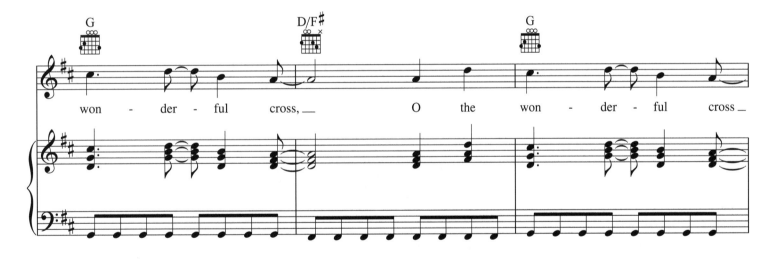

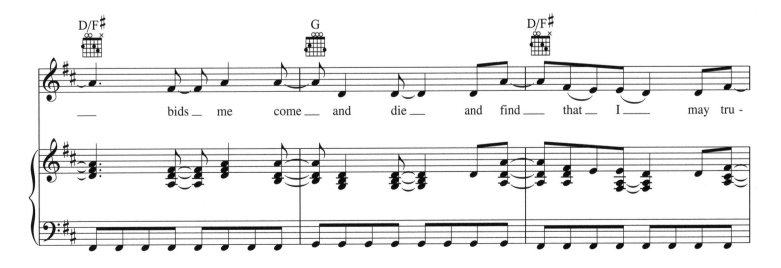

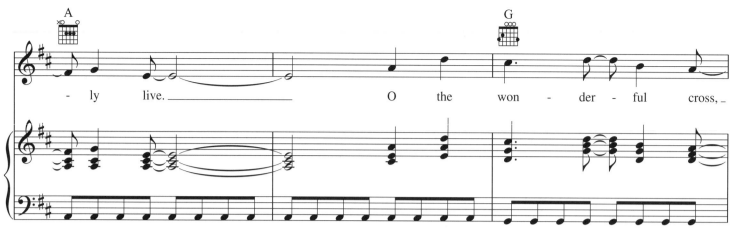

-ly live._____ O the won - der - ful cross,_

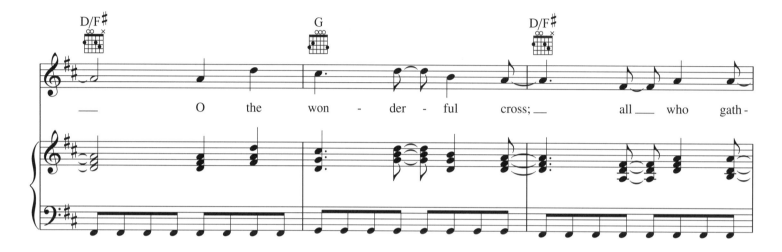

__ O the won - der - ful cross;__ all __ who gath-

-er here __ by grace __ draw __ near __ and bless __ Your name._____

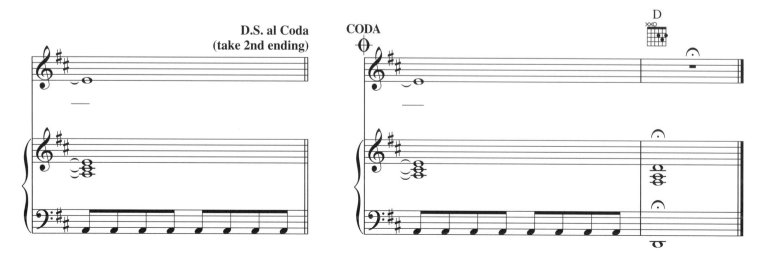

D.S. al Coda
(take 2nd ending)

CODA

YOU ARE MY KING

(Amazing Love)

Words and Music by
BILLY JAMES FOOTE

I'm for-giv - en ____ be - cause You were ____ for-sak - en.

I'm ac-cept-ed; You were ____ con - demned. ____ I'm a - live ____ and well; ____ Your

Spir - it is ____ with-in ____ me be - cause You died ____ and rose ____ a - gain. ____

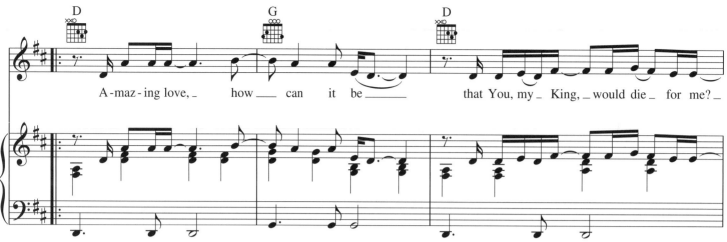

A-maz-ing love, _ how _ can it be _____ that You, my _ King, _ would die _ for me? _

_____ A-maz-ing love, _ I _____ know it's true; _____

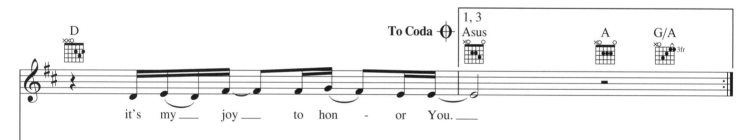

it's my _ joy _ to hon - or You. _

To Coda ⊕

1, 3

2

_____ In all _ I _____ do, _ I hon - or You. _

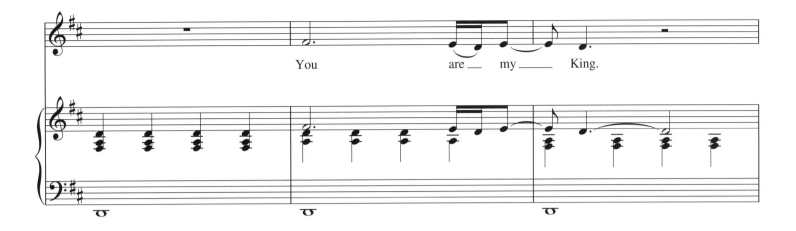

You are my King.

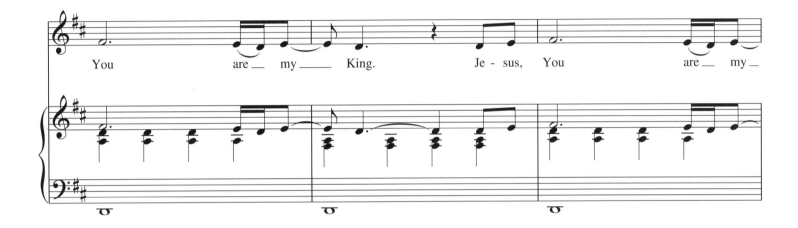

You are my King. Je - sus, You are my

D.S. al Coda
(with repeats)

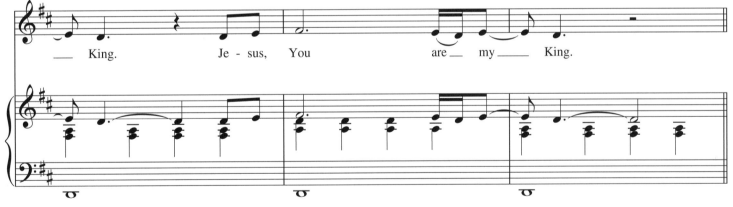

King. Je - sus, You are my King.

CODA

| Asus | A | G | A | D |

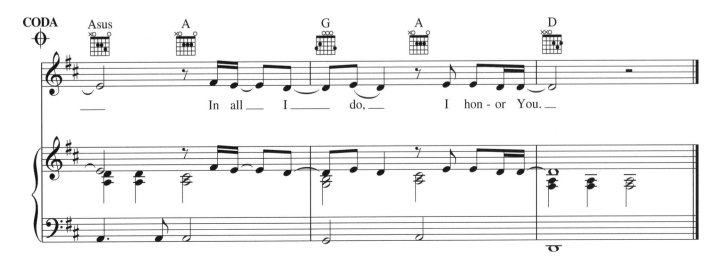

In all I do, I hon - or You.

WORTHY IS THE LAMB

Words and Music by
DARLENE ZSCHECH

Thank You for this love, _____ Lord. _____ Thank You for the

nail - pierced hands. _ Washed me in Your cleans - ing flow, _ now

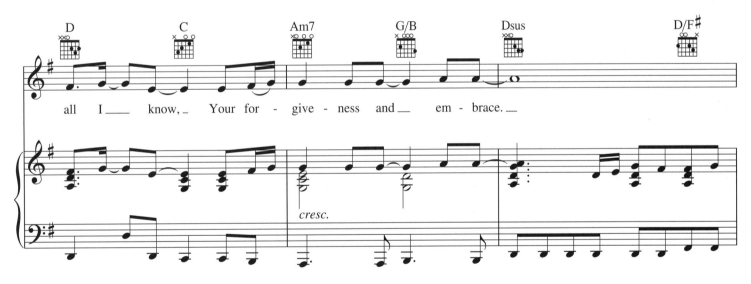

all I __ know, _ Your for - give - ness and __ em - brace. _

Wor - thy is __ the Lamb, _____ seat - ed on __ the throne. _

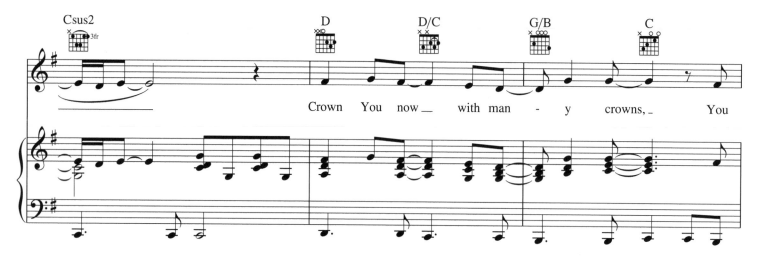

Crown You now __ with man - y crowns, __ You

reign vic - to - ri - ous. __ High and lift - ed up, __

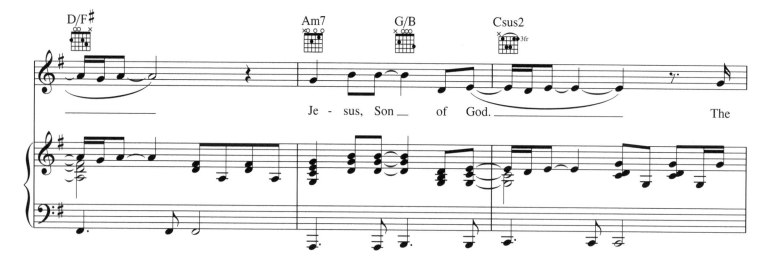

Je - sus, Son __ of God. __ The

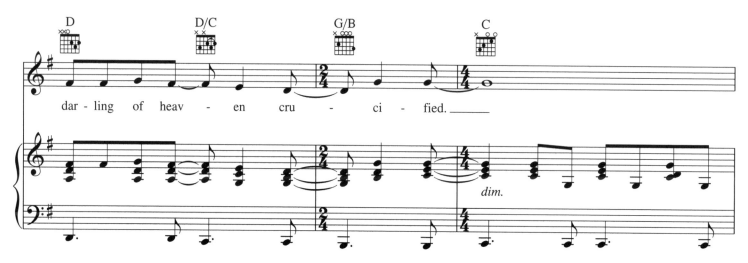

dar - ling of heav - en cru - ci - fied. __

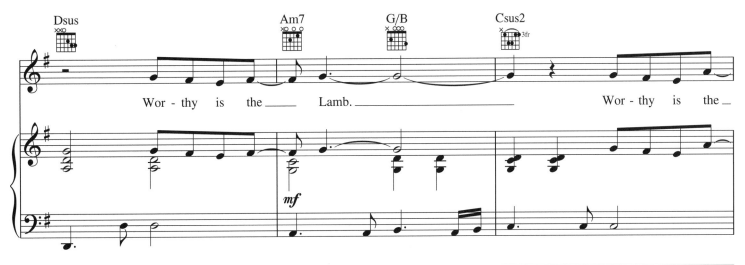

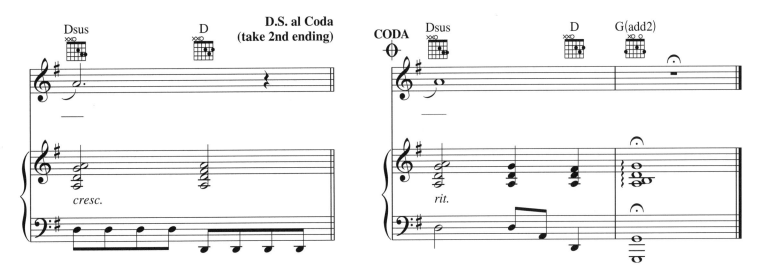

YOU GAVE YOUR LIFE AWAY

Words and Music by PAUL BALOCHE
and KATHRYN SCOTT

Gentle Ballad

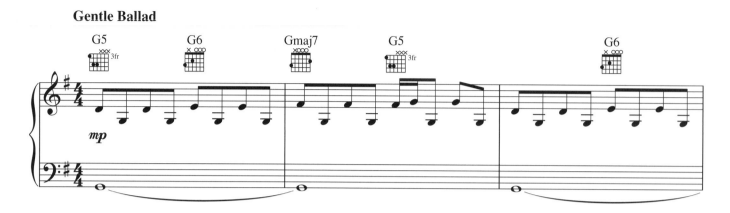

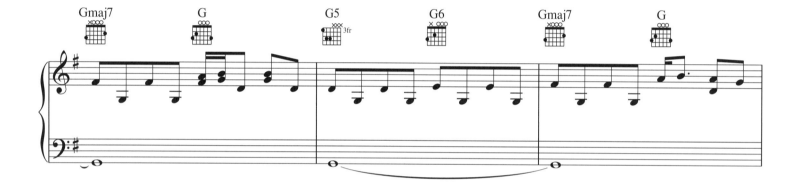

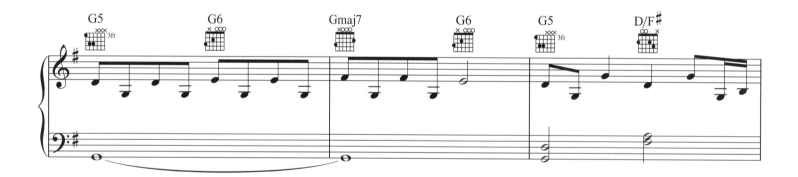

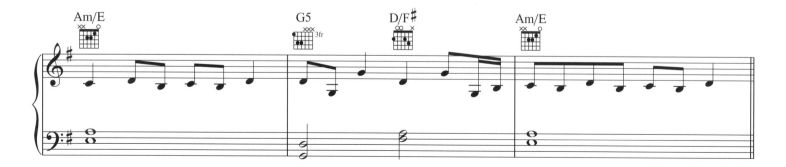

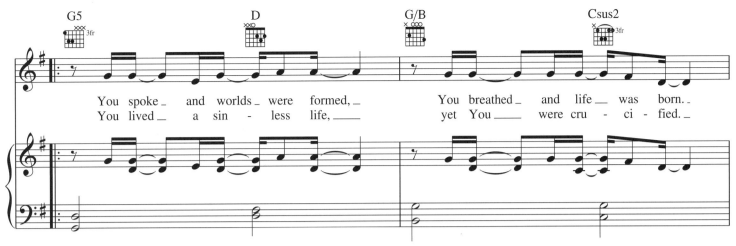

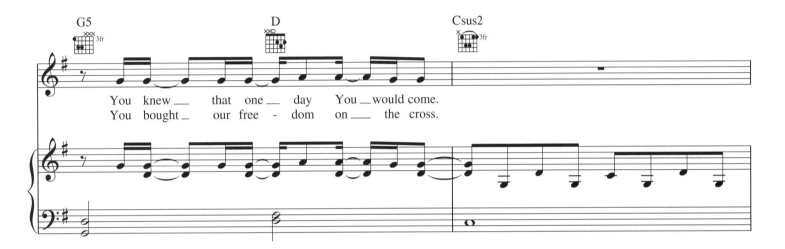

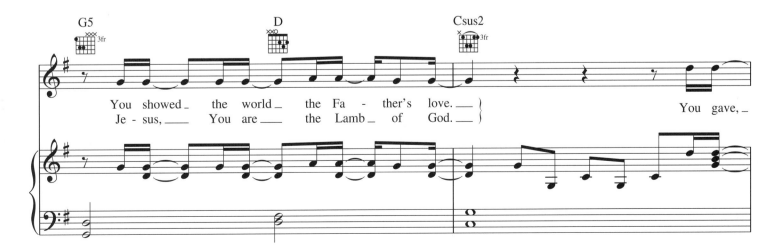

You gave_ Your life_ a - way. You gave,_ You gave_ Your life_ a - way. You gave,_

You gave_ Your life_ a - way for _____ me. Your grace_

has bro - ken ev - 'ry chain, my sins_ are gone,_ my debt's_ been paid. You gave,_

You gave_ Your life_ a - way for _____ me, for _____

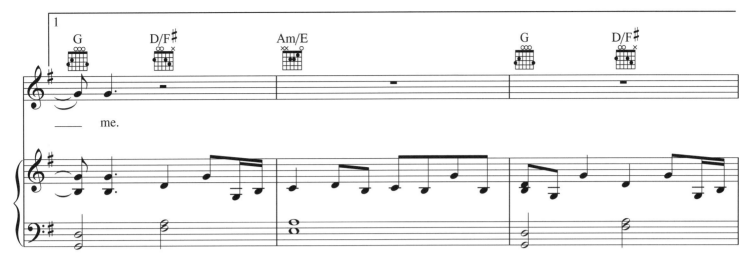

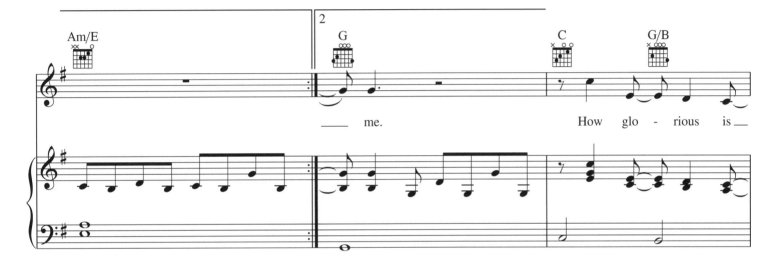

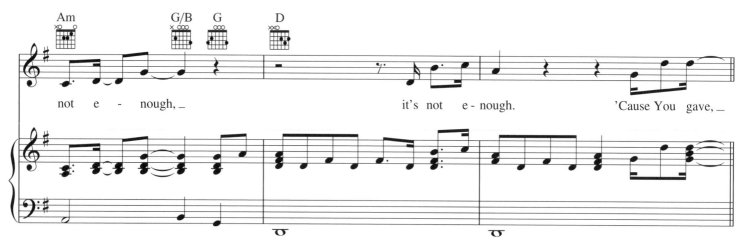

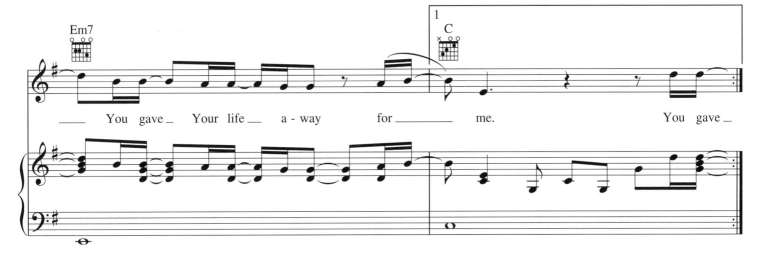

You gave__ Your life__ a - way for_____ me. You gave__

__ me, for_____ me.

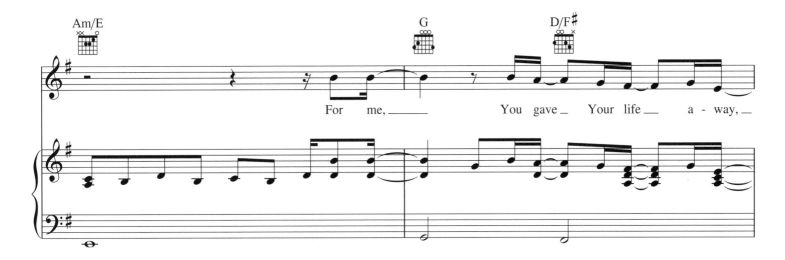

For me,_____ You gave__ Your life__ a - way,__

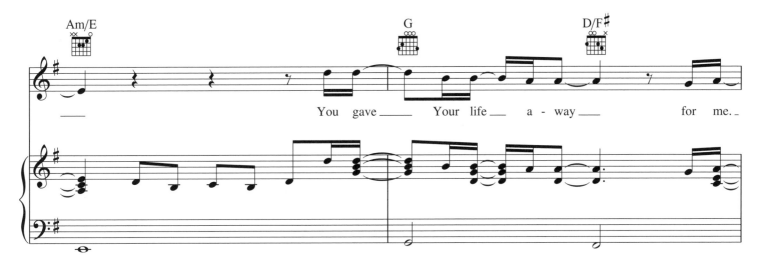

__ You gave_____ Your life__ a - way___ for me.__

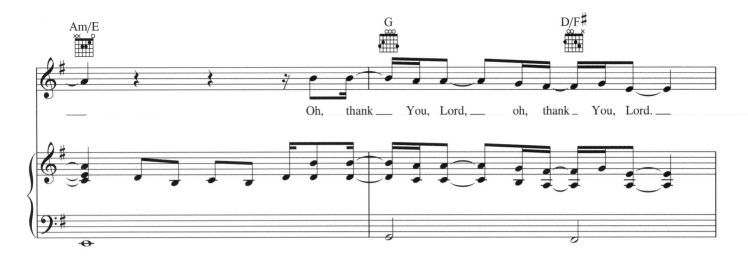

Oh, thank__ You, Lord,__ oh, thank__ You, Lord.__

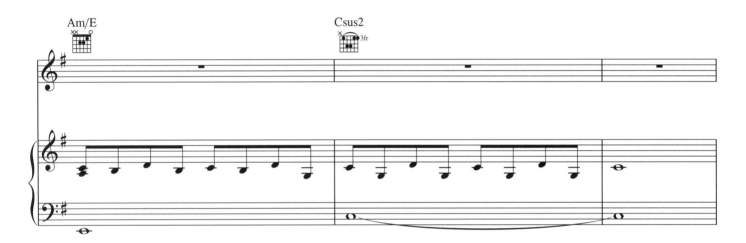

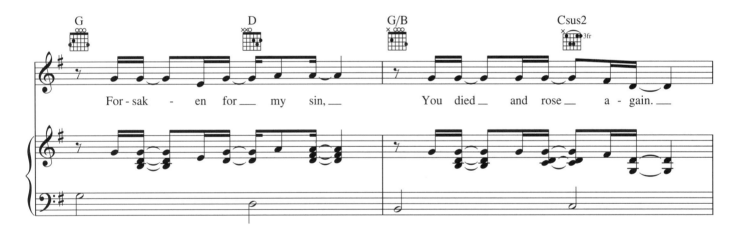

For - sak - en for__ my sin,__ You died__ and rose__ a - gain.__

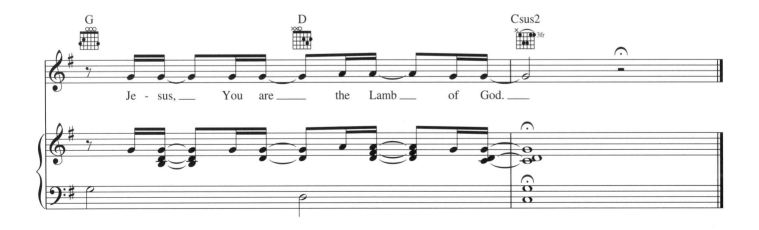

Je - sus,__ You are____ the Lamb__ of God.__